FACING THE
BLACK SHADOW

By Marlene F. Watson

Copyright © Marlene F. Watson, 2013
ISBN: 978-0-9889201-1-8
Cover Illustration by Sylvia L. Walker,
Copyright © Marlene F. Watson, 2013
Cover design by Michael Leclair

All rights reserved.

Without limiting the rights under copyright reserved above, no part of this publication may be reproduced, stored in or introduced into a retrieval system, or transmitted, in any form, or by any means (electronic, mechanical, photocopying, recording, or otherwise), without the prior written permission of the copyright owner.

The names and identifying characteristics of people quoted in this book have been changed to protect their privacy and confidentiality.

If you like this book, tell your friends! For comments, questions and more information about upcoming books and appearances by Marlene F. Watson, visit www.drmarlenefwatson.com

Dedication

This book is dedicated to The Creator,
Who is no respecter of persons.

The Ancestors,
Who wished for freedom.

My Late Grandmother, Mandora Beckett Watson
Who inspired me to write this book.

My Mother, Verneda Martha James
Who was always there.

My Niece, Anique Brittany Clements
Who personifies grace and beauty.

My Nephew, Gary DeShaun Collins, Sr.
Who got another chance.

Acknowledgements

With heartfelt gratitude, respect, and affection, I thank the following people for coming along on the journey to *Facing the Black Shadow*: My clients and students, thank you for the lessons you taught me and for being courageous.

My aunt Velma Virginia Rhodes, thank you for being my cheerleader.

My rock, Milton A. Dunton, Sr., thank you for your unwavering love and faith.

My siblings, Brenda K. Collins, Keith B. James, Harry R. James, Jr., and Sherry F. Hales, thank you for being you.

My nephews and nieces Gary D. Collins, Sr., Lamont R. Collins, Keith James Gibson, Gregory Clements, Jr., Tariq Vinson James, Anique B. Clements, Jayda N. James, LaShaun M. Collins, Lamont R. Collins, II., Lamere Collins, Jayvon Collins, Jeanetta Collins, and Gary D. Collins, Jr., thank you for being beacons of hope.

My sister-friends who gave encouragement, Argie J. Allen, Erlene Berry Wilson, Stephanie Stokes Oliver, and Denise Ray-Shields, thank you for your enduring friendship and support.

My dynamic duo: agent Regula Noetzli and editor Laura Markowitz, thank you for being so wonderful.

Artist and illustrator Sylvia L. Walker, thank you for getting it.

Readers, Drs. Paulette Moore Hines, Rona Preli, and William L. Turner, thank you for your precious time and honest feedback.

Table of Contents

Introduction 1

Chapter 1
The N-Word and the Black Shadow 10

Chapter 2
The Myth of Black Inferiority 33

Chapter 3
The Black Family: For Better and Worse 58

Chapter 4
Black Women Through the Lens of Slavery 78

Chapter 5
Shadow-Boxing with the Boy 97

Chapter 6
Casting the Shadow over Intimacy 120

Chapter 7
Divided over Class 142

Chapter 8
Dismantling the Collective Black Box 157

About the Author 172

Introduction

I am three years old and running barefoot in my grandmother's colorful garden, giggling as I chase the beautiful butterflies that are drawn like magnets to the red, white, pink, yellow, orange and lilac colors of the flowers. It's a summer day and I feel the freedom of wearing nothing but panties to cover my bottom. I have no worries. I am safe and secure, surrounded by people who care about me.

I hear my name. "Faye-eeee!"

Somebody's calling me. It's my grandmother!

I run inside to see what she wants, and wait – slightly winded – while she sits calmly on the sofa with her cup of hot tea. She is listening expectantly for the train to rattle the china closet as it roars past the house. This is a daily ritual that we both love. I sit beside her. As the train nears, we hear the first sound of dishes shaking. She says, "Brazolia's here."

Greedy for the compliment that I know is coming, I wait for it with anticipation. "You're pretty, just like my sister Brazolia," she tells me.

I feel like Snow White, the fairest of them all.

Decades later, I sit on another sofa with my beloved grandmother and I can't believe my eyes. Her brown skin is barely touched by age, but her once-long black braids are now thin, grayish-white plaits that hang limply down her back. What I notice are her eyes, which aren't seeing me. Dementia clouds her mind, and she talks to herself in a stream of consciousness that makes no sense. But then my heart skips a beat as I hear her mutter: "I was never pretty like my sister Brazolia. She was the pretty one. I was black and ugly."

I'm shocked. Did my beautiful, vibrant grandmother truly believe that? I had never heard her put herself down before, but maybe it should not have been such a shock. Everyone knew that in her family, her younger sister, who looked nearly white with straighter hair and lighter skin, was the center of attention. Relatives would come to town to see her, and on their way back they would stop in the road in front of my grandmother's house and say, "We'll have to catch you the next time," and I would see the pain flash for a moment on her face before she smiled and waved. She never said a negative word about her relatives, but once, as an adult, I heard her tell a story about one of her older brothers holding her hand to the fire and saying she was black anyway, so it wouldn't make a difference. She carried the burn marks on her hand.

I took my beloved grandmother's hands in mine and looked straight into her pained eyes, willing her to live forever. As she looked back into my eyes, addled with dementia, I imagined a conscious part of her was trying to say, "Bear witness for me, Faye. Tell our people what the black shadow did to me, and what it's doing to us."

The black shadow is a burden every black person carries, whether or not we are conscious of it. It lives deep in our unconscious minds and influences us all the time, and we are neither aware nor mindful of its profound influence on every aspect of our lives. What is the black shadow? It's the running inner dialogue we have with ourselves all day long about our fears of being inferior as black people. It is our internalization of the white man's lie that blacks are inferior to whites – the very lie that was the foundation of our ancestors' enslavement. The black shadow is more than simply internalized racism; it's also our complex feelings of fear and despair about being black, and consequently our longing to be less black.

From the moment we're born, we're judged by the color of our skin, just as our parents and their parents were. No black person escapes the black shadow because racism is part of the air we breathe in white-dominated America. But we can learn to bring it into the light and face it – expose the lies it feeds our own minds and hearts. That's what this book is all about: understanding the black shadow and its influence on our feelings, choices, beliefs and soul so it will no longer have power over us.

If you're having a hard time picturing your black shadow, think of that bad feeling you get when you walk into a meeting late and all eyes are suddenly on you and you feel judged for being black, not for being late. That is your black shadow. It makes you self-conscious about being black because it tells you constantly that being black means you are automatically ugly, inferior and every other enduring stereotype of the "lazy nigger" that was created during slavery. The black shadow makes every experience of rejection, failure and disappointment more bitter because it reinforces the belief that these negative outcomes are inevitable and deserved simply because one is black. The black shadow tempers experiences of success and joy with conflictual feelings. You can imagine it as a bully in your own mind who is constantly ready to put you down and make you feel small, beat you up and mock you. That is the job of the black shadow, which is a multigenerational legacy passed down from slavery.

I am well aware that talking about slavery is something that makes many African Americans extremely uncomfortable, and I want to admit up front that I do intend to talk about it in these pages, because in my opinion it is the root cause of the lie of black inferiority. In my therapy office, I hung a painting on my wall showing black slaves picking cotton. I knew some of my clients would find it provocative, and I was curious to see who would remark on it. After his third session, a high-powered black attorney finally brought it up.

"Why do you have that in your office?" he asked, a challenge in his voice.

"I think it's important to acknowledge our history and be connected to it," I replied. "Does it bother you?"

"I don't like it," he admitted.

I asked him why he chose to speak about it now. He explained that he was having problems at work. His efforts were being devalued by his white boss, and he felt like he would never be valued as highly as his white colleague no matter how hard he tried. So he didn't want to sit in my office and be reminded of slavery and blacks picking cotton because he didn't want to feel the same helplessness and inadequacy. He was an educated, affluent, well-employed black man. He was worlds away from the reality of his slave ancestors, yet his inner struggles were echoes of theirs. He had a daily, low-level insecurity that his white boss saw him as nothing more than a well-dressed "nigger." Underneath the appearance of unshakable self-assurance, his black shadow undermined his sense of self-worth.

Our racial memory of slavery and the instructions we were given to become "nigger" in order to stay alive takes us away from our true selves. We're not true to our own intelligence, spirit, strength and character because the black shadow is in our heads criticizing us and knocking us down all day long. The black shadow not only undermines our self-esteem and self-confidence as black people, but it also feeds on our desire to be accepted by whites; our fear that we'll always be inadequate; our despair and hopelessness that this situation will never improve. The black shadow is a menace to the mental health and happiness of every single

INTRODUCTION

African American and our multiracial brothers and sisters. However it's so ingrained in us and has been with us our whole lives so we don't even realize it!

How did the black shadow manage to get such a strong grip on our psyches? Why are we so twisted up inside our own heads with the idea that we're inferior because our skin is dark? It's no great leap to trace the black shadow back to slavery. Although slavery happened to our ancestors and not to us, it left holes in our families, in our histories, in our identities and in our ability to feel valued for our intrinsic humanity. Since the first African slaves were kidnapped and taken to the New World, black people in this country have internalized the messages of black inferiority. Over many generations, blacks accepted the lie that dark skin makes a human being inferior to light-skinned people. But what makes the situation even more distressing is that we, the descendants of slaves, also inherited a culture of silence around slavery.

Every spring, Jewish people celebrate Passover, which commemorates the Exodus from Egypt. They have a ritual meal called a *seder*, during which they talk about how their ancestors were slaves. Jews say, "Once, we were slaves to Pharoah in Egypt," as if it happened to them, personally. When a Jewish friend described this to me, I laughed to myself imagining what would happen if I invited a bunch of my African American friends and family to dinner so we could talk about slavery. No one would show up!

I don't know any African American family (including my own) that has openly and willingly discussed slavery's invasive impact on our relationships with self, other African Americans, other people of color and/or whites. Even though slavery ended 150 years ago, it remains a shameful and painful subject for most African Americans, causing us to join the white chorus in declaring that slavery is irrelevant to contemporary African Americans. Most of us don't even know our own family histories because those stories about the days of slavery (which lasted hundreds of years!) are not seen as fit for discussion. Juneteenth celebrations, when they happen, don't dwell on slavery, but focus on emancipation. The only ritual I know from slavery is jumping the broom. Even Kwanza, a ritual that grows more popular with African Americans each year, has nothing to do with slavery, but reaches back to pre-slavery African principles.

"Let's leave it in the past," a client once said to me when I tried to bring up for discussion the legacy of slavery in her family.

But the bitterness, sadness and trauma of slavery are still very much with us in the present, in the form of our black shadows. Most of us can't bear to watch movies about slavery, let alone have a heart-to-heart talk about our feelings about it, but this should not be seen as a personal failure by African Americans. It is merely an aspect of the continuing legacy of slavery that we inherited. The fact is, slavery still impacts us, whether we're willing to talk about it or not. Let's stop colluding with the denial and prolonging the silent grieving that cannot be addressed because we decendents of slaves won't talk about it. Let's name this undercurrent in the achievement gap between whites and blacks. Let's dare to really heal.

I can just hear what the skeptics are thinking: "If we open up that can of worms, it will just make things worse."

How can it get any worse? More than 400 years of wallowing in guilt, shame, moral outrage, blame, anger and finger-pointing has left us stuck, and our people still have not healed from the wounds of slavery. Rather than dodging meaningful conversations about slavery, we should welcome the opportunity to understand how slavery institutionalized an enduring system of white superiority and black inferiority (white gain and black loss). Once we acknowledge that slavery is the cracked foundation of America as the land of opportunity and justice for all, we can take steps to understand how white superiority and black inferiority function on both a personal (black shadow) level and larger institutional systemic level.

The black shadow was created by slavery and it persists today as a kind of personal enforcer of racism. This sounds like bad news, but I promise you this is a book of hope. As a family therapist who has worked with hundreds of clients and met hundreds more at conferences and workshops on racism, I have personally witnessed the black shadow being exposed and transformed into a tool to help black people live emotionally richer and happier lives. I have witnessed this in myself, as well, so I can speak first-hand about how to get there. At the end of each chapter, I offer exercises you can do alone, with your family and with your friends and loved ones so that you can start your own healing. *Facing the Black Shadow* will teach you how to become conscious of how our black shadows operate to keep us from knowing our authentic selves and connecting to one another and our history with open hearts.

INTRODUCTION

African Americans are aware that our mere presence – our blackness – activates negative racial stereotypes in whites, but we are far less aware of how it activates negative racial stereotypes in ourselves. While strolling with my honey in downtown Johannesburg, South Africa, a young black man who was hanging on the corner with his boys pointed at Richard as we walked by. Then he said loudly, "He a real nigger. Hey! Gimme some money, nigger!"

As this young man took hold of Richard's arm, I crossed the street to get in a waiting taxi. When Richard caught up to me and asked, "Why'd you leave me?" I answered that I didn't want to be bothered with such "foolishness."

At the conscious level of my thinking this was true. But on the unconscious level, I didn't want to be associated with "nigger." Richard was "nigger" and I didn't want it to rub off on me. The black shadow had made me abandon my companion out of fear that being with him would make me a "nigger" too. It was a painful, but important, revelation for me. I realized that when I feel uneasy in my black skin, or accuse other blacks of making the rest of us look bad, or attempt to elevate myself by separating myself from my brothers and sisters, or even embrace and act the part of "nigger," it's my own black shadow rearing its head. In Chapter One, I examine how the fear of "nigger" controls black people and feeds the black shadow.

African Americans are constantly being taught that black means "inferior." In my therapy practice, I help African American families and individuals understand how the internalized belief that "black" means "inferior" overshadows our decisions about what we can and can't achieve, who we can and can't be, and who we can and can't love. In Chapter Two, I look at how the myth of black inferiority permeates our psyches and influences our choices, helping the black shadow maintain its power over us.

When we look in the mirror, the black shadow whispers to us, "You're too black. You'll never be beautiful. You're unworthy of love." My mother, who now has Alzheimer's, stands in front of the mirror in her bedroom while she rubs her skin and accuses her image of being black.

"How did I get so black? Why am I so black?" she asks, confused and distressed. The first time I saw her do this, I was horrified! I tried to comfort her.

"Mom, you're dark. I'm dark. We're supposed to be dark because we're black people!"

It doesn't comfort her. On her dresser sits a photo of my biracial niece, Jayda, who will turn six this year. She's half Italian, half African American – fair-skinned with soft, curly hair. My mother stares at that picture and says, "She's so beautiful." All her grandchildren are beautiful, but my mother singles out this little one because she has light skin and "good" hair. In Chapter Three, I explore skin-tone privilege and the pain and rejection we create and perpetuate by our own internal family racism, which stems from our unconscious belief in the myth of black inferiority. In Chapters Four and Five, I take this to the individual level, looking at the masks men and women wear to try to shield themselves from the painful fallout of believing that blacks are inferior. And in Chapter Six, I examine male-female intimacy and the places where we get stuck because of our black shadows.

The black shadow gains power when black people are divided. In Chapter Seven, I describe black class issues and point to the ways our black shadows influence us to fight among ourselves rather than uniting to fight racism. In Chapter Eight, I continue this thread with a discussion of what I call the "collective black box" – the self-selecting groups we create in the black community that exclude those who are different from us. Why our black shadows pressure us to reject our own community members involves complex psychological dynamics. I describe them in the hope that becoming conscious of the problems they cause will motivate us to become a community that embraces diversity rather than needing black individuals to conform strictly to black shadow social norms.

For one brief moment, the election of President Barack Obama offered hope for healing as a nation from the wounds of slavery. Many black and white people had not expected to see a black president in their lifetimes, and his decisive election seemed like a dream. But soon after he took office, racist images of the first black president and disrespectful cries, such as "You lie," by House Representative Joe Wilson of South Carolina brought us all back to reality. The post-election climate of the United States under a black president was our surest sign that we need to talk about slavery and the myth of black inferiority.

INTRODUCTION

Slavery is an American story, a story of violence, pain, injustice, loss and grief for African Americans. To be white was to be human and normal; blacks were not fully human; we were the despised "other" and treated as far inferior to whites. Slavery marketed the idea of black inferiority. Slavery encouraged black visibility (the "other") and white invisibility (the norm). Still today, white invisibility obscures white privilege, while black visibility affirms black inferiority. Consequently, whites internalize white privilege and blacks internalize black inferiority.

It's slavery that created the black shadow, and it is up to whites and blacks to examine white privilege and black inferiority and to commit to ending slavery's hold on each one of us. Since this is a book about African Americans written by an African American woman for all who have the heart and courage to hear and – I pray – the will to work hard to undo the legacy of slavery, we'll be talking about eradicating the black shadow from the hearts and minds of black people.

For everything, there is a season, and African Americans need a season now to grieve and heal from our history of slavery. Any therapist can tell you that unresolved grief creates big problems – addictions, depression, illness and more. But many people still want to avoid grief. They mistakenly believe that grief is a never-ending process, a kind of eternal mournfulness. The kind of grief recovery I'm talking about is not that at all. It's about completing the process of grieving, which our ancestors were not allowed to do, so that we can integrate the truth of what happened into our lives and move forward without the burden of unfinished business.

African Americans need a season now to feel and be compassionate toward their own pain before the healing process can begin. Slavery takes some sitting with to understand what it did and is doing to us and how we really feel about it. Some of us are descended from the white people who owned our ancestors, and these genealogies are confusing and disturbing. Many of our family stories have been lost forever. Even so, we need to sit down and have the conversations. *Facing the Black Shadow* will help you start the conversation in your own mind, and then, hopefully, you can start them with your beloveds. When we face and transform our black shadows, we will finally close the wound of slavery. We will have peace in our lives and an open heart for others.

I know that African Americans already have too many battles – for social and economic justice, for respect and dignity and safety in our families and communities. We get tired just trying to survive each day, and the thought of fighting some shadowy mental process might feel like one task too many. If you're tempted to put this book down, I urge you to read on, because this fight against the black shadow is one you *can* win, because *you* have all the power. You *can* change your own mind! You *can* weed out the negative voice of the black shadow, once you understand where it comes from. I've been a therapist for 35 years, and I've worked with countless African American individuals, couples and families dealing with every kind of life issue. I have seen them heal and live happier lives by confronting their own black shadows. It really is possible, and I have faith that you can do this. I have faith that you will truly be able to be happy once the black shadow stops running your life.

Chapter 1
The N-Word and the Black Shadow

When I was a girl, my grandfather liked to tell me the story of Tar Baby. It's a popular folk tale that was passed down through the generations in the storytelling traditions of people of color. There are 300 versions of the story and in Africa, India and the Caribbean, Tar Baby is also part of the literary tradition. I believe it has a lot to teach us about the relationship between the black shadow and the N-word. (For a book of folk tales, I recommend *The People Could Fly: American Black Folktales told by Virginia Hamilton.*)

The story is about Bruh Fox, who constructed Tar Baby (a figure made from tar) to catch old Doc Rabbit, who'd been drinking all of his cream. When Doc Rabbit spied Tar Baby, he tried talking to him. But when Tar Baby ignored him, Doc Rabbit decided he was stuck up. This made him fighting mad, and Doc Rabbit kicked Tar Baby hard with one foot. Of course, it immediately got stuck in the tar. Doc Rabbit was so mad that he kicked him with his other foot, and now both feet were stuck. Doc Rabbit was so consumed with rage that he ended up with his whole body stuck in Tar Baby.

Tar Baby is analogous to the word "nigger." Because Doc Rabbit is unable to recognize the truth that Tar Baby isn't real, he gets trapped in the lie. Likewise, the N-word traps African Americans in the lie that "nigger" – shorthand for black inferiority – is true. This lie is the fertile soil that nourishes the black shadow. Doc Rabbit also gets trapped by his need to be acknowledged by Tar Baby. We get trapped by our desire not to be "nigger," yet it's still the measure against which we judge ourselves and others. (Further down in the chapter, I'll be talking about the problems this causes us.)

The word "nigger" is an agent of the black shadow, and it stalks and hounds every black one of us – including our multiracial brothers and sisters. Please understand: it's not just a word. "Nigger" was a deliberate tool of enslavement wielded by white slave traders and the racist society that colluded to make slavery possible. It's been used as a weapon for centuries to keep us in line, keep us down, keep us in our place and make us feel ashamed. To say it's just another racial slur, or only a disparaging label for dark-skinned people is to ignore its poisonous history. The N-word was a shorthand way for whites to refer to our slave ancestors as subhumans. Along with the whips and the chains, it was how white society enforced slavery's imperative of black inferiority. When uttered by a white person, it labeled the black slave as a sub-human: dirty, shiftless, ugly, worthless, lazy piece of property. Whether it was used casually, or with overt malice and scorn, the N-word provoked in most blacks intense feelings of shame, helplessness, suffering and despair. The N-word was a burden our slave ancestors carried, and the wounds it left were not as obvious as the lash. The concept of "nigger" took root in their psyches. They were so miserable, so beaten down that they couldn't help but wonder if the white man was right about their inescapably "nigger" natures. Maybe being black did make a person less capable, less intelligent, less talented, less beautiful – inferior to the white masters in every way.

One of the enduring tragedies of slavery is that these doubts, and the label "nigger," were passed down from generation to generation not only by whites, but also by blacks. As a family therapist, I know that multigenerational messages are most often unconscious, which means they go unchallenged. The misguided beliefs and behaviors are simply accepted as "normal" in the family. It takes a crisis for someone finally to name the dysfunction and stop the cycle so it doesn't continue in the next generation. But until these unconscious messages are challenged, they can eat away at the soul of a person, a family, a community. There is no doubt that all of us who are descended from slaves have, to some extent, internalized the white oppressor's lies about us. The little voice in our heads that whispers, "uppity nigger" when we dare to have ambitions is the black shadow we carry inside. Its constant undermining of our confidence and self-esteem serves to reinforce the white man's lie that no matter how educated, how wealthy or how respected we are in the world, we'll always be "niggers."

"Not me, Marlene!" I hear you thinking. I hope that's true. I know from my therapy practice, and from my own life experiences, that many of us are in denial about how deeply we're affected by the black shadow. But I also believe

CHAPTER 1 – THE N-WORD AND THE BLACK SHADOW

that some black people have shaken free of their black shadows and been able to disassociate themselves from this kind of negative, self-destructive thinking. If I didn't believe it was possible, I wouldn't be writing this book! My supposition is that most black people are still struggling, and it is for those readers that I've written this book – to help you find your path to face your black shadow and take back the power and pleasure it saps from your life.

"Stop Talking About Slavery!"

It's very hard for us to admit that the slavery of our ancestors has an impact on our lives today. Slavery was so unimaginably horrible that naturally we want to dissociate ourselves from it and claim that it doesn't affect us. But there's no way we will ever be free of the black shadow if we don't face slavery's residual effects on us and understand the ways it affects our psychology. We live in the land of our ancestors' enslavement, a land where the history of slave trade, slave ownership and slave abuse is swept under the rug because it makes white people uncomfortable. They prefer the myth of America as the land of the free and home of the brave. They don't like the ugly truth that the founding fathers owned slaves; that all settlers in the New World profited and benefitted from black slavery; that slavery was justified as an honorable and economically savvy institution because dark-skinned people were seen as less-than human. The psychology of the enslavers and the entire white society that allowed slavery to exist was built on three factors: greed, objectification and hatred. Economic self-interest drove whites to embrace slavery. But in order to convince themselves that there was nothing wrong with it, they had to objectify black people – see them as inferior objects. Hatred and even fear of blacks reinforced the psychological loop, allowing whites to continue objectifying and exploiting black people. All of this made four hundred years of slavery possible.

The psychological ramifications of the silence, and the continued racism we dark-skinned people experience in the United States, are woven through every part of our lives: how we raise our children, who we desire, who we trust, the hopes we allow ourselves to have for ourselves and our loved ones. We might not be in physical bondage anymore, but psychologically, African Americans are still oppressed by the black shadow.

The black shadow is a psychological dynamic. It's a way of thinking and responding to the world from a deep-seated belief in the inferiority of black people – ourselves included. It tells us we're "niggers": ugly, worthless, defective and undeserving. The black shadow's domain is our unconscious minds, so when we think these negative thoughts about ourselves and other blacks, or when we make choices or act out from these beliefs, we're not aware that it's the black shadow poisoning our minds. That's a huge problem, because it means we simply accept that our critical, judgmental, rejecting thoughts and actions are correct and even appropriate. In this unconscious way, we limit ourselves and censor other blacks. We let our belief in "nigger" and our fear and shame at being thought to be one, rule our choices and behavior.

If we could only become aware of the black shadow and name it, it would lose its power over us. The good news is that we can! This book is all about how it can be done. The first and most crucial step is to become aware of it. The black shadow is the thoughts in your head that intimidate and control you by holding the fear of "nigger" over your head.

The N-Word: Should It Be Reclaimed?

Internalized racism is the unconscious acceptance of society's prejudices, biases and stereotypes of one's own racial group. In other words, we African Americans have absorbed all those low expectations and negative ideas about "niggers" and in an unconscious (and sometimes conscious) way, we believe them. That's one aspect of the black shadow. Another aspect is our desire to be accepted by the rejecting society; fear that we will always be inadequate because we're black; hopelessness that we will never be free of this fear and desire; and confusion about how to survive under the hostile conditions of racism. If you wonder why your life isn't happier or easier, or why you haven't achieved more, remember that the black shadow constantly undermines your self-confidence and saps your energy. It's hard to be truly free and happy with the black shadow riding you day and night.

That's one reason why I believe the N-word triggers such intense reactions when it's used by someone who isn't African American. It echoes – and reinforces – the black shadow we already carry inside. One of my clients came to therapy one week highly agitated. He recounted what had happened a few days earlier:

CHAPTER 1 – THE N-WORD AND THE BLACK SHADOW

"Driving to work this white guy in a jeep cut in front of me. I pulled up beside him at the next traffic light and said, 'Hey, be careful. You almost caused an accident.' I wasn't mad, just concerned. He looked at me, said 'Fuck you, nigger!' and sped off. I got so mad I could hardly see straight. I took off like a nut trying to catch him, but I couldn't. Then as luck would have it, I saw him in the employee parking lot when I got to work. I fucked him up good."

Although it was originally a Latin word used to denote the color black, "nigger" has become one of the most toxic words in the English language. It's potent enough to make a peaceful person like my client turn violent.

I know what you're thinking: "If it's such a toxic word then why do so many black people call one another 'nigger'?" In the 1970s, popular black comedians including Richard Pryor and Paul Mooney made it a black household word, and it was picked up by other entertainers. When hip hop and rap became popular, the word went viral. Tupac is credited with using "nigga" in song, but in interviews he explained that for him it was an acronym for "Never Ignorant Getting Goals Accomplished." This may have been a creative attempt to reclaim the N-word and transform it into something positive for black people, but the word fell short of Tupac's vision, as witnessed by the number of young black men and women in prison, on drugs, or dead – including Tupac, himself. Comedian Chris Rock defines "nigger" as a "low-expectation-having motherfucker." Although he means to be amusing, I believe that's a truer reflection of how African Americans relate to the N-word in their innermost hearts and minds, and so I find his use of it sad rather than funny.

"Niggers ain't shit," I hear black people say.

"Nigger" means you are implicitly inferior by virtue of being black. Even if no one ever defined the word for you, you learned this at your mother's bosom. The lie of "nigger" is bone deep, programmed into our thinking and reinforced by the white world and white culture and by other blacks and black culture.

"That's a fine nigger!" a black woman says as an attractive black man walks by.

Think about what we're saying about a man when we say that. A "fine nigger" was the black slave who was the master's sexual stud – a breeder who could increase his master's wealth by impregnating female slaves. He was an object, a possession; not a human being.

My job as a therapist is to help people who are struggling to understand why they're in so much psychic pain, and why their lives aren't turning out the way they'd hoped. Having heard, time and again, how often African Americans are "low-expectation-having," I don't believe we can reclaim the N-word and take back its power. I understand and sympathize with efforts to take the sting out of the N-word by using it in comedy or as code for black solidarity. It makes sense that we'd want to try to neutralize a word that has been used to put us down and keep us in our place by dangerously powerful and malicious adversaries. But if you really absorb the terrible history of that word, no black person should want to call someone or be called a "nigger." Maybe someday, when we're able to talk openly about how slavery still has an impact on us today, we'll be able to reclaim the word. But I don't think we'll want to.

Let's understand that using the N-word isn't reclaiming it. Casting off the black shadow starts with facing the harm "nigger" does to our psyches. Our denial and resistance to looking at the N-word this way, is part and parcel of our community's deep taboo against talking about slavery among ourselves and with the wider world. Seriously, the N-word is still a weapon of racism that cuts us down. You use it at your peril, because the N-word serves the black shadow. (For a complete history and exploration of the word nigger, I recommend the book *Nigger: The Strange Career of a Troublesome Word* by Randall Kennedy.)

The Dangers of "Ghetto"

Many of us joke about one another's "ghetto" ways. The adjective "ghetto" is simply a more socially acceptable way of labeling someone a "nigger" when we catch him or her engaging in objectionable and threateningly "nigger" behaviors. These might include speaking grammatically incorrect English, dressing "ghetto-fabulously" (flashy clothes draped with bling), having a lot of family members living in same house, baby-mama drama, etc. A best-selling humor book, *150 Ways to Tell If You're Ghetto*, advises readers on what is and isn't ghetto. For instance, "You know you're ghetto if you have a wife and kids but still live with your parents." It's like the *The Official Preppy Handbook,* which lampoons WASP behavior. But there's actually a big difference between the two, because it isn't dangerous for WASPs to bear that label, and it can, in fact, increase their prestige in the world. Not so for someone labeled "ghetto," because the word is shorthand for "nigger."

CHAPTER 1 – THE N-WORD AND THE BLACK SHADOW

I know humor can be a resource for coping with adversity, but the label "ghetto" (despite the authors' disclaimer that a person of any race can be ghetto) has everything to do with color in a world where black people are the "niggers" who live in ghettos. Both "nigger" and "ghetto" carry the same negative connotations. Should we joke about absentee black fathers and by doing so imply that there's some genetic (racial) flaw in black men? If we do, we're reinforcing society's denial that slavery has anything to do with it. Boys learn the roles and expectations of manhood from their fathers, so consider that our men are still influenced by the roles they learned as slaves when they weren't allowed to know – much less parent – their own children. Joking about "ghetto" glosses over the fundamental reason our families have struggled for generations with fracture and violence. We have to take personal responsibility, of course – I'm not saying we should give absentee fathers a pass because their ancestors were slaves – but without understanding how the black shadow controls us, we aren't free in ourselves to make better choices.

Contemporary media offers a constant barrage of negative stereotypes of blacks. These negative attitudes are directly linked to the racism that we experience every day, and each one has roots in the "nigger" lie that traces back to slavery. Black people who use negative stereotyping in their art, entertainment, scholarship and elsewhere are letting their black shadows speak the lie. White America likes it when we make fun of ourselves. It makes them feel safe – we're not angry, we're funny! In the same way feminists were dismissed by men as having "no sense of humor" when they challenged gender discrimination (which is not exactly a humorous topic), blacks are often criticized for being too "angry," as if this is our problem and not a direct response to systematic discrimination.

The black shadow makes it possible for us to believe white America's criticism that we shirk personal responsibility by blaming all our problems on race or on the fact that we're descended from slaves. Consequently, African Americans have little insight into the way we internalized the notion of black inferiority from slavery. If only we could face our history of slavery head-on and come to terms with its effects on our lives, we would benefit in every way. We would value our abilities, believe in ourselves and one another, and be able to find more joy in life.

In 1979, after a trip to Africa, Richard Pryor announced that he wasn't going to use the N-word on stage anymore. We can follow his example. Let's refuse to inflict the N-word on one another ever again. Together, we can start to dismantle the lie of "nigger" and embrace the truth about ourselves. Black people are brilliant, talented, innovative, strong, beautiful and a gift to the world.

Bearing the Collective Burden

When Timothy McVeigh was arrested for bombing the federal building in Oklahoma City, thin white men around the country who wore jeans and t-shirts didn't worry that they would suddenly be viewed by random strangers as potential terrorists. When you're black, you know that whites will judge all of us based on one person's bad behavior. Black people are all seen as suspect when one black misbehaves, from holding up a liquor store to making too much noise in a restaurant. Consequently, blacks are on constant alert when it comes to monitoring the behavior of other blacks – what I call bearing the collective burden. The astronomical cost to us for being on "black watch" is self-rejection, individual alienation and group separation.

Bearing the collective burden is a survival mechanism, but it's also a manifestation of our fear of being seen as "nigger." I was reminded of this one afternoon when I lunched with a white colleague at a restaurant. The white couple sitting near us was loud, ill-mannered and excessively demanding of the waiters. Had they been black, I'm sure my black shadow would have made me unconsciously sink a little lower in my chair and feel embarrassed for all black people by their "nigger" display. I glanced at my colleague to see if she was embarrassed by these ignorant whites. She wasn't! She even found them amusing, because it never occurred to her that two socially inappropriate white people would reflect badly on her and all white people. Whites never have to think about being called "nigger," no matter how ignorant their behavior seems to us blacks. There's no equivalent word in the English language that implies white inferiority.

That experience stands in stark contrast to an encounter I had in a grocery store. An older black man and I witnessed a young black mother hurl curses at the back of her son's head. I understood where the older man was coming from when he hung his head and said, "Sometimes I wish I wasn't black."

I felt his pain and his shame. I knew that feeling of dread that I was being judged for the behavior of another black person. The black shadow's voice in my head was running through black stereotypes. I recalled a saying from my childhood: "Niggers and flies I do despise."

CHAPTER 1 – THE N-WORD AND THE BLACK SHADOW

As soon as I became aware that I was having that thought, I told myself, "You know better!" But I was still worried that the white people in the store would look at me the same way they were looking at that abusive black mother. I was momentarily ashamed of being black, and I was also ashamed of my black shadow.

It comes up all the time, for all of us. I hear it from my clients; I see it in myself. There was that surge of disapproval I felt recently when I saw a black couple dressed in matching red suits. Somewhere, I'd been taught that red isn't a "respectable" color for blacks because it's flamboyant and calls too much attention to dark skin. Then there was that Sunday jazz brunch in Philadelphia at the trendy, upscale restaurant Zanzibar Blue. That brother across the room sure was fine, but why'd he have to get all loud, yelling out his appreciation of the bass player? And what about the time I refused to date a very nice African American cab driver because his English was substandard? In each of these instances, I was uncomfortable because of my projection of the black shadow. I defended myself from becoming "nigger" by rejecting these black brothers and sisters. If the "other" is a "nigger," then I – the one pointing the finger – am not, right?

We have a greater chance of connecting with our collective strengths instead of defining ourselves by our collective weaknesses when we openly and honestly talk about our feelings of shame and fear as black people. But honest and open conversation is difficult because of the black shadow. Anticipating white censure, we judge ourselves and one another too harshly.

The "Nigger" Scapegoat

In Biblical times, a scapegoat symbolically carried away all the sins of the Hebrew people. In modern times, the "nigger scapegoat" is our way of dumping all the sins of being "nigger" on one person and then distancing ourselves from him or her, thus proving that we're not "niggers." We punish those who don't act, talk, dress, behave and speak in a manner that's acceptable to whites. This self-censorship of the community is our black shadow at work. It warns us to dissociate from the offending "nigger" before the stink rubs off on us.

Fear of becoming the "nigger scapegoat" – of being censored by our own community – isn't something we are conscious of. Working on us behind the scenes, the black shadow fills us with fear and judgment and keeps us from questioning the white lie that shaped the whole concept of "nigger." All we know is that it's bad to be judged a "nigger" by other blacks. As long as we remain unconscious of the black shadow, we will continue to limit our expression of emotions and individuality and shun diversity within our own community. (I will talk more about this in Chapter Eight).

As a therapist, I know how dangerous it is for our psychological, physical and spiritual well-being to squelch these feelings. Repressed feelings have a way of coming out in ways that are harmful as they lobby to get our attention. On my own journey to confront my black shadow, I had to face my fears of being judged a "nigger" and come to understand where that fear comes from and what sustains it. The social meaning given to the word "nigger" – lazy, shiftless, dumb, broad-nosed, big-lipped, nappy-headed, dirty, and violent – is inflammatory and our psyches want to wipe off the black and smear it onto someone else. I found safe places to have honest and open dialogues with other black people who could help me release this burdensome belief in black inferiority and then grieve for how much energy and joy it had drained from me during my lifetime. I was lucky to have support and a faith community to help me. I knew the black shadow was keeping me from being the whole and loving person I wanted to be, and that knowledge motivated me to do the work of bringing the black shadow into the light so it no longer had the same power over me that it once did.

The Origins of the Black Shadow

As Chinese general Sun Tzu wrote, "Know thy enemy." So where and when did the black shadow originate? Somewhere between Africa and the Middle Passage, during the 16th to the 19th centuries, the black shadow was born and took root. This was, of course, the period when trade in African slaves flourished. During the journey from their homes in Africa to the slave markets in the Caribbean and United States where they were ultimately sold, each black man, woman and child was transformed from a human being into a "nigger." It started with how they were viewed and treated by the slave traders. The white slavers couldn't afford to acknowledge the humanity or individuality of the Africans they had kidnapped or bought from other slave traders. The captives' feelings and thoughts didn't matter. The captives' languages, names, customs, beliefs, rituals, tribes and roots were irrelevant to the white thieves, who were interested only in their bodies to perform work or to breed more slaves to increase the white masters' wealth. The white men inured themselves to the human suffering they were creating by regarding the "niggers" as no different from horses, cows or other livestock.

Further complicating the picture was the truth that some Africans were sold into slavery by their own or other tribal leaders. In one account I read, a woman was sold by a tribal leader to a white slave trader for the price of three cotton handkerchiefs. So in addition to the dehumanizing treatment by the white slave traders, the African slaves also had to process the horrible betrayal of their own neighbors and elders.

In this cauldron of trauma, grief and despair, the black shadow was born. Besieged by culture shock, powerless, isolated, mourning the loss of family and home, the African captives were enslaved. They were deprived of all but the barest essentials of life, subjected regularly to physical, sexual and emotional abuse, separated from beloveds – including their own children – and denied rights, resources, education and hope. Over time, and over generations – this went on for three hundred years – African Americans unconsciously (and sometimes consciously) came to accept the master's definition of them as "nigger."

Comprehending the Psychological Effects of Slavery

Psychologically speaking, the fallout of slavery was devastating. Just think of all the losses: love, trust, connection, belonging, sense of identity, self-esteem, freedom of expression, control over one's own mind and body. It wasn't safe for a slave to feel emotions. It wasn't safe to face their grief or allow their feelings of fear, sadness, rage or hopelessness to show. It took all their energy and wits to survive in a new and strange land, living as a "nigger" and as the property of others. Learning to be a "nigger" was necessary for the slaves' survival. It was what the white man expected, and pleasing the white man increased a slave's chance of survival. Slaves who let their white overlords see their intelligence, talent, ambition and self-esteem were typically punished for forgetting their place – for forgetting they were "niggers."

The black shadow found its way into our ancestors' psyches in the cargo holds of the slavers' ships, but it was on the plantations and in the fields and in the masters' houses that it took root and passed itself on to future generations of African Americans. The training of blacks to survive in the white world by accepting "nigger" – accepting the lie of black inferiority – still affects us today. Today, our brothers and sons are taught to be meek and nonthreatening when in the presence of police officers and other whites in power so they won't be punished for being "niggers." They have to dress a certain way or risk being viewed as dangerous, as happened, tragically, to Florida shooting victim Trayvon Martin. He was shot by a neighborhood watch member simply because he was wearing a hooded sweatshirt and therefore looked like a criminal to the shooter. Because of the black shadow, we continue to convey to young blacks – consciously and unconsciously, through "nigger scapegoating" and other reprimands – that they must appear nonthreatening to whites in order to raise their odds of survival. That might mean telling them not to speak up when they feel they are being treated unfairly, or not to draw attention to themselves by being "too loud." The worst sin they can commit is to be an uppity nigger, meaning too smart, competent and unafraid of the white man. When he was running for president, Barak Obama's critics accused him of being "elitist," which is just another way of telling a black man he's an "uppity nigger."

Trauma had a tremendous impact on the psyches of our enslaved ancestors. We hear about soldiers coming back from war with Post-Traumatic Stress Disorder, which is a condition of acute anxiety. People who suffer from traumatic stress have a hard time moving on with a normal life because they haven't found ways to resolve the traumas they experienced. They need a safe place where they can talk about what happened in order to start to heal. The African slaves who were brought to America to be tortured, starved, raped, abused and worked to death never had that safe place. They couldn't talk about their losses. Therefore, they couldn't resolve their trauma, and so it burrowed deep in their hearts, minds and spirits and came out in other self-destructive ways.

If you're having a hard time imagining how this works, I'll tell you about one of my clients. Carmen, a senior in high school, was brought to therapy by her mother after discovering that Carmen had an eating disorder and was cutting her arms and thighs with a razor. She'd been doing it for months and hiding the scars with long pants and long sleeves. A classmate had seen the cuts and told the guidance counselor at their private school. The classmate also said that Carmen had mentioned killing herself a few times. When the guidance counselor contacted Carmen's mother, the mother had a hard time believing it because at home Carmen appeared happy, always joking and laughing. She was a talented tennis player, had friends and brought home good grades. It was inconceivable to the mother that her daughter would want to hurt herself.

I was curious about the timing, and wondered if Carmen was feeling anxious about leaving home in a few months to start college. After she and I built a trusting therapeutic relationship, the reason for her self-cutting finally came out. Carmen revealed that she had been molested by her grandfather at the age of 9, during a summer vacation at his house. The little girl never told anyone because her grandfather was revered in the family and community. She couldn't express all the traumatic feelings she had about being abused – betrayal, fear, sadness, anger – so Carmen buried her feelings in binge eating and throwing it all back up. Now, she was preparing to go away to college because that's what was expected of her, but she was terrified of leaving home. She had not left home since she was 9, and that was when this terrible thing had been done to her.

Our minds are not always logical and linear. As a small child, she blamed herself for the abuse. Everybody said her grandfather was a good man; therefore, she must have been the bad one. It must have been something she said or did that made him turn into a terrifying monster and hurt her so brutally. As she grew older, a rational part of her mind knew the abuse wasn't her fault, but a doubt persisted: maybe she really had done something to make him violate her. Maybe she really was at fault.

It doesn't take much of a mental leap to imagine that the messages of "nigger," reinforced day in and day out for centuries, would fill our slave ancestors with self-doubt. Like Carmen, a part of them must have believed they were at fault. Like Carmen, they would have had a terrible inner dilemma: they would believe the lies of the abuser, but they would also know in their hearts that they were human beings deserving of respect and dignity. What happened to Carmen is a tragedy, but thankfully her parents got her the help she needed to heal. If she hadn't, she might have grown up to be an anxious mother, terrified to let her children out of her sight, or rejecting of her daughters when they turned 9 because they reminded her of herself at that age when something terrible had happened to her. We don't always know how unresolved trauma will manifest, but it's never healthy when it does. That's why it was so vital that Carmen talk about it, understand the truth of her experience and forgive herself for not telling anyone when it happened. Only then could she truly heal and move on. The urge to cut herself and the eating disorder disappeared and she went off to college and had a wonderful experience.

Unfortunately, our ancestors didn't have the freedom, the resources or the safety to heal from the multiple traumas they experienced. The black shadow is our inheritance from the unhealed wound of slavery – unhealed trauma passed down from generation to generation. I see evidence of it all the time in my therapy practice. It's hard for black people to feel safe enough to talk about their real feelings. Like Carmen, they find it easier to deflect those feelings into self-destructive behaviors. When I hear African Americans joking about the N-word, I wonder if they are deflecting their feelings of horror and sorrow at the truth about slavery. It's clear from how our community reacts to the suggestion that we discuss slavery (we run the other way!) that we don't feel safe enough yet to face what slavery did to us and how it makes us feel.

So let me thank you right now for reading this far into my book despite my insistence on talking about slavery! I imagine some people will already have put it down, saying to themselves, "Why does she have to dredge up that old history?" It takes courage to face the terrible things that happened to our ancestors. There were an estimated 12 million Africans shipped to the Americas in chains, and each one of those individuals lost everything they cherished. That's a massive amount of loss and trauma, and ensuing generations born into slavery faced the challenge of never having known freedom, and one imagines they had even fewer inner resources to resist the black shadow.

Missing Branches on the Black Family Tree

You may still have a hard time understanding what I mean when I say that we are still affected, in the 21st century, by the trauma and loss of slavery. Let me try to make that clearer for you. In family therapy, we first get to know clients by drawing their genograms. Picture a multigenerational family tree, and now include all kinds of information such as alliances and cut-offs among family members; addictions and abuse; migration, incarceration and college graduation. What we look for are patterns that are passed down from generation to generation, and we always find them. It's not mysterious: we learn about relationships from our families, and

CHAPTER 1 – THE N-WORD AND THE BLACK SHADOW

when we grow up and have families of our own, we naturally repeat some of those same patterns even if they were dysfunctional.

African American genograms have gaping holes – empty branches on our families' trees – because we inherited a multigenerational tradition of fractured families. Our slave ancestors were not allowed by the white masters to marry, although some were fortunate enough to be able to stay with a beloved and maybe even "jump the broom." Their children, however, belonged to the master and often were sold off. Men were used as breeders, forced to impregnate women at their master's command. Women were not only regularly raped and impregnated by black men at the command of the master, they were also raped and impregnated by their masters and white overseers. That's still a very difficult topic to talk about in the African American community. How confusing and uncomfortable to hate the oppressor – and to be related to him.

Those born into slavery typically didn't know who their parents were. They may have been sold many times and moved from master to master. So much vital information was lost: the names of their parents; the name and place of the tribe their forefathers and foremothers belonged to; the names they were given by their birth mothers.

These gaping holes and unspoken questions represent a mind-boggling loss for each one of us. My white clients can take pride in their heritage. They will happily tell me how they inherited their musical abilities from this great-grandparent, and were named for an ancestor on that side of the family, and how six generations back their people came from some European country, and they've been back three times to visit the old family home. In contrast, African Americans can't trace back more than a few generations. The blank branches on the tree need to be talked about, need to be mourned, but it's hard to express the sadness and bewilderment we feel at not knowing our own roots. Ironically, we feel ashamed about it.

Wait a minute! Why should we feel ashamed? It's white society that allowed slavery and profited from it.

Our shame comes from the black shadow. It intimidates us so that we won't delve into this subject matter. It doesn't want us to look at slavery because slavery is the root of its power. It's more than happy to tell you right now, "Close the book! She's talking about slavery and all that nonsense again. You don't need to think about that. It has nothing to do with you."

Don't listen to your black shadow. It's time to make yourself available for healing. As a famous poet once wrote: "The best way out is to go through it."

Understanding the Roots of Black Shame

It's hard to admit that we're ashamed of being black. I came of age during the Black Is Beautiful era of the Civil Rights Movement, and we fiercely claimed our black pride. But shame is the black shadow's specialty, and none of us escapes it to some degree. One example of extreme shame was a graduate student I mentored several years ago, I'll call her Angela, who was African American but told everyone she was Latina. Angela's own self-rejection resulted in her alienation from other African American women in our department. I was concerned about her, and invited her to talk to me about what was going on. She told me she didn't like African American women because they didn't accept her as a Latina. Instead of challenging her assertion that she was Latina, I talked to her about the black shadow and internalized racism. Eventually, Angela admitted that she was African American. She said it had been difficult being a black girl in her primarily white high school so she started lying about her heritage. The few other black students in her school knew she was lying and felt resentful and disrespected. They shunned her, which made her feel more alienated. Instead of being angry at racism, she took her anger out on other blacks, who represented what she was ashamed of in herself.

Shame is a powerful problem that black and multiracial people grapple with. We judge ourselves constantly and feel ashamed when we don't measure up. Do we have light-enough skin? Too-dark skin? Good-enough hair? Bad hair? Do we speak "proper" English or Ebonics? Are we black middle class or black underclass? We also shame one another with our debates about who's black and who's not, and we cause our brothers and sisters to feel they don't belong in the community because they're not black enough.

When we don't recognize how shame rules us, we end up very unhappy. I worked with a middle-aged man, Joe, who told me that he viewed black women as being unclean. He dreamed of finding a young, thin, blonde, white woman to marry. He struggled with feeling uncomfortable and impotent in his black skin, but he was sure he would finally feel like a real man once he made love to a white woman. As we explored his feelings, he came to realize that he believed having a white woman as a lover would somehow prove that he was an "exceptional" black man – meaning not a "nigger." In his lighter-skinned black family, it was common to talk down about other black people. They regarded themselves as not having much in common with blacks. Joe's desire to be validated by a white woman was an attempt to erase his "nigger" shame.

Joe worked on overcoming his prejudice against blacks. I remember once he told me that he knew I was black when he first called me because of the way I talked. "You sounded black," he said, implying that there was something wrong with this. He also proudly pointed out that no one would know he was black by the way he spoke. I offered him a new way to look at his problem, framing it in terms of the black shadow. What would be so wrong about someone on the other end of the telephone knowing that he was black? He became aware of how his black shadow constantly sneered at him for being black and made him feel like he was really just a powerless "nigger" and not a real man at all. I coached him to challenge the black shadow by staying aware of his thoughts and rejecting the ones that were clearly sending him the message of black inferiority.

The black shadow sneaks into our consciousness no matter how ferociously we defend against it. When a black woman is outraged that a black man is with a white woman, the black shadow is activated, whispering to her that a black woman is a "nigger," born to be raped, bred and abused. She's black, and therefore not entitled to be treasured by any man, especially her own. When a black man prefers only light-skinned black women, his black shadow is acting out. He doesn't know why he's attracted to light-skinned women. But his black shadow knows that it's an attempt to camouflage him – *the no good, low-down, dirty "nigger."* Like my client Joe, these men secretly believe that having a light-skinned woman on their arms when they venture out into the world makes them more acceptable and respectable, meaning more white and less black.

When a black mother berates her child in public or at home for "acting like a damn fool" when he or she is being a normal, wiggly kid, the black shadow is speaking. The mother shames her child out of embarrassment and also to train her child not to be a black person who draws attention to his or her blackness. She wants the child to be safe, and she wants the child not to embarrass her. She can't name what has suddenly come over her. But the urge to stop her child from acting like a "nigger" is unmistakable. The black shadow makes her lash out at the child with hurtful vehemence. In the end, she might feel ashamed, and on top of that she still feels like a "nigger" woman with a "nigger" child. That is the face that stares back at her when she looks in the mirror of society.

Me and My "Nigger" Self

The black shadow manifests powerfully in our young people. On every street corner where young black men hang out you can hear the call of the shadow demanding attention as they cry out, "Yo, nigger," in greeting to one another. The young brothers attempt to wrest control of their pride and self-esteem from their black shadows using reverse psychology. They use the N-word to take the power back from it – or at least they try to. Just using the word doesn't erase the centuries of shame and doubt planted in the "nigger" inheritance that is theirs now.

These young men remind me of He Lion in the tale of "He Lion, Bruh Bear, and Bruh Rabbit." The story goes that He Lion walked around roaring, "Me and Myself!" all day, which scared all the other animals in the forest. He Lion wasn't going to let nobody tell him what to do. He wasn't afraid of the Man that Bruh Rabbit said was the real king of the forest. After thinking on it, He Lion agreed to go along with Bruh Rabbit and Bruh Bear to see the Man. He Lion roared, "Me and Myself! Me and Myself!" to remind himself who he was, and then they set off on their journey.

Bruh Rabbit was smart. He knew to be afraid of the Man. And Bruh Bear was smart enough to take Bruh Rabbit's cautions to heart about the Man. When they found the Man, Bruh Rabbit and Bruh Bear jumped into the bushes to hide. But the proud He Lion stuck his chest out big and walked right up to the Man. The Man was glad to see He Lion's chest up close. It made his job of shooting He Lion all the easier.

Reverse psychology doesn't work when it comes to the N-word. The white man didn't just come up with a word; he concocted a tale of the big, black, scary nigger monster who needs to be mastered or put down. And the white man made sure he had the power and the means to keep the "nigger" down. So young men who act "nigger" and try to become the big, black, scary monster the white man invented are no wiser than He Lion sticking his chest out big in front of a cocked gun. The proof is in the alarmingly high mortality rates of young African American men. It's in America's prisons, which are permanent home to a staggering number of has-been He Lions with black shadows that roar, "Me and My *Nigger* Self."

"*Here I am twenty years old and sitting in a cell now for three years and shit… But you know white people have a lot of pitfalls set up that distract us from searching for the truth. They be having us playing them Supernigga roles.*" (Flyy Girl, by Omar Tyree)

The White Man Within

The black shadow doesn't just make us get down on ourselves for being black, it compares us, constantly and unfavorably, to whites. We internalize the notion that whites have positive characteristics and blacks have negative characteristics. This is what I call "the white man within." The voice of comparison and criticism is so ever-present that we don't recognize it or stop to challenge it. The inner dialogue of the black shadow is all about how we don't measure up to whites. It tells us: White people are decent and upstanding with good values and morals. Black people are evil and out to do harm. White people are smart. They invent amazing things and have more intellectual prowess. Black people are ignorant, slow, lazy and suited best for menial work. White people keep their neighborhoods nice. They care about cleanliness and tidiness and order. Black people ruin their own neighborhoods with broken glass, garbage and graffiti, and they mess up a nice place with their dirty ways. White people have money and they can buy nice things. Black people can't manage money and don't deserve nice things. White people work hard and achieve their goals and ambitions. Black people are lazy and don't have any goals or ambitions.

My client Joe and student Angela went so far as to disown their blackness because of this "white man within." Ashamed of being black, they judged their own people harshly, as they imagined white people judged them – as they judged themselves, because of the voice of the black shadow telling them blacks are inferior.

If our ancestors had never been enslaved by chains, and later by the white man's "nigger" lies, how might we think about ourselves and other blacks differently? Our failure to recognize the white man within causes us to do the white racist's work for him. When black people see a black mother with a child, we assume she's single and irresponsible. When we see a young man in a hoodie, we assume he's a gang-banger. Watching a TV interview with a rapper, I caught myself thinking, "Wow! This guy is smart!" I'd assumed he wouldn't be because he was dressed "ghetto" and so I lowered my expectations. When we see homeless black people on the street, we say to one another, "They're just lazy and looking for a handout." When we see whites on the street, we wonder if they're returning war vets who need help. We can have goodwill toward whites, but not blacks!

The black shadow clings tightly to African Americans. Any manifestation of Negroid features – skin color, hair, nose, lips, body type – or cultural traits – soul food, music, dance, laughter, speech, manner of worship – or any other detail associated with being black is enough to trigger our fears of being "too black." Likewise, any deviance from the cultural stereotypes, (*"All black people can sing and dance,"* and *"All black people eat black-eyed peas and grits"*) is enough to release our compensatory guilt for not being black enough. Both reactions are opposite sides of the same coin, resulting in black people having an unrealistic expectation of sameness for one another. The expectation that blacks are a homogenous group keeps blacks both connected to, and isolated from, one another. Black people were estranged from one another by slavery, led astray by the oppressor with one word: "nigger."

Reconnecting with Slavery

After years of listening to the black shadow speak through the mouths of my clients, and hearing it in my own head day after day, I made a commitment to expose and banish my own black shadow. I started by reading books. I read slave narratives and other historical material on slavery. To be sure I didn't distance myself from their painful stories and minimize their accounts as fictions that had nothing to do with me, I spent time imagining that I was them, and in this way I formed a spiritual connection with the people whose stories I read. I felt a bond to each one, and silently thanked them for having the courage to talk about their experiences so we African Americans in the future would understand. Fully embracing those voices helped me start to overcome my shame about my own black shadow because I realized that all the compassion I was feeling for those long-dead slaves I could also feel for myself.

Reconnecting with slavery is vital to our recovery. Remembering that slavery is the cause of our shame and fears will give us the confidence we need to face the black shadow and change our behavior. Finally grieving for what was taken from us and done to us by our history of slavery will help us to develop a spirit of kindness and cooperation in our own community. Learning from the traumatic events of slavery, we will become desensitized to being judged a "nigger." Moreover, realizing the burdens caused by slavery's transformation of us into "niggers," we can finally commit to rid black America of the "N-word." The black shadow is fated to reappear in the lives of our children and in the lives of our children's children if we don't correct our distorted thinking and promote healing through discussion of slavery.

What Changes When You Confront the Black Shadow

When I began to face my own black shadow, I noticed that it had less and less power over me. It was subtle at first, but there is one example that stands out. A white colleague told me that he preferred to collaborate on a project with a different black colleague because she smiled and I didn't. If I had heard that comment before I'd done this work on my black shadow, I would have felt furious with my white colleague, but also ashamed with myself for not earning his approval. I would have felt competitive with my black colleague and also anxious. But having confronted my black shadow, I didn't immediately feel shame and internalize his comment as my black failure. Instead, I was able to evaluate his comment critically and realize that he assumed that it was my job to make him feel comfortable, and by not smiling I was rejecting that as my role both as a woman and a black person. Instead of seeing my black colleague as a rival for his approval, I enlisted her as an ally. I recounted the conversation with her and we had a mutually supportive talk about how to respond to white male expectations of black women to take on the "Mammy" role of nurturer and ego-booster. I mentioned reading about how our ancestors who were house slaves competed with one another for acceptance by the powerful whites, and she understood that I was saying I didn't want to do that, or to feel divided from her, and she didn't either. Instead of judging each other, we accepted the beautiful truth that we are two separate individuals with our own unique personalities, and her way of being a black woman and mine are both fine.

In the past, the black shadow made white people's problems with me my problems, but I don't get hooked that way anymore. It's delightful! A heavy burden has been lifted from my heart and mind.

Exercises
Start Your Own Healing Right Now

You can get started right now facing your black shadow. Here are a series of conscious things you can do to start exposing the black shadow and healing from it.

Step 1: Clarify how you feel about the N-word. Write down all the negative things the N-word stands for. Read it aloud. How does it make you feel?

Step 2: Talk to your children about the N-word. Encourage children to explain their thoughts, feelings and emotions about the word. Promote new rules of communication with family and friends by challenging them to avoid use of the N-word.

Step 3: Stop laughing at the N-word. Build turst and support among family and friends so they won't have to mask their real feelings in humor and sarcasm.

Step 4: Don't withdraw from family members because they act "ghetto." Promote understanding and acceptance of black diversity. Don't give the N-label to blacks when they behave in ways in which you don't approve.

Step 5: Think about our lives before slavery and the N-word. Visualize black America without the N-word. Imagine that you are back in Africa, safe in your village, where you hear good talk about your people. Fast forward to the future where you're sitting in a movie theater watching a black movie, and the N-word is not uttered by one black person, on screen or off. Feel how calm and relaxed you are with the burden of "nigger" removed.

Step 6: Remind yourself that our ancestors fought for our right to be free of the N-word, some of them sacrificing their lives. Write down five things that represent the sweetness of freedom to you.

Step 7: Develop a family plan for not using the N-word. Make not using the N-word a common family goal. For every week you go without using it, put ten dollars in a "Family Fun Fund."

Step 8: Celebrate your accomplishment. Have a family celebration with the Family Fun Fund when you go ten weeks without using the N-word.

Step 9: Evaluate how you and your family cope with racism. Develop a plan of action for responding to racism, including advocating for your children against racism.

Chapter 2
The Myth of Black Inferiority

The black shadow is fed and powered by the myth of black inferiority. The internalized belief that blacks are less worthy than whites impacts how we think about ourselves, how we perceive one another and our sense of unity in the black community. It underscores all our relationships. Internalized black inferiority can be embarrassing and make us feel even more inferior. One client summed it up very succinctly: "I'm ashamed of being black, and ashamed of being ashamed of being black." He concluded by saying, "It's all fucked up."

But where do we learn that blacks are inferior? If you're thinking, "Everywhere!" then of course you're right. Growing up in a racist society, African Americans are put under a microscope and judged constantly, not as individual human beings, but as blacks. And it's not just the white world that judges us; we also learn to judge ourselves and one another. We constantly scrutinize how we talk, what we wear, what we eat, how our children behave, and we judge ourselves and others as being "too black" or "not black enough." But do we realize that each time we do this we're teaching ourselves to believe in black inferiority?

I had an interesting conversation with a client one day when she came in with a new hairstyle – twists. I complimented her on her gorgeous new look. She thanked me and then out came the confession: "I felt so bad yesterday after going natural that I wrote about it in my journal last night. It's the new millennium and I still have baggage about black inferiority."

I said, "You're one of the fortunate ones because you recognized it and used your journaling as a management strategy." It's being unaware about it that hurts us the most.

In Chapter One, we examined the black shadow's deep roots in the white slavers' lies about black inferiority. In this chapter, we're going to look at how we can dismantle our own internalized belief in black inferiority, which is what gives the black shadow power over us.

Black Inferiority Development

You didn't wake up one morning and suddenly believe blacks are inferior. This lie has been passed down from generation to generation among blacks and whites. How did it even start? It evolved in developmental stages.

Stage One: *Loss of Self-Identity*

The first stage began with slaves losing their self-identity. In my readings about Africans who were taken captive and sold into slavery, I was surprised to learn that those individuals didn't think of themselves as "black." Each one was tribe-identified. The slavers stole their tribal identities and even took their given names from the Africans they enslaved. There's a powerful illustration of this in a scene from the movie *Roots*. Kunta Kinte is tied to a tree and whipped because he insists on keeping his African name. The white slaver beats him until finally when he asks, "What's your name?" Kunta Kinte answers, "Toby."

Prior to slavery, blacks didn't view skin color as a defining factor of human worth. But to make slavery work, white people had to strip every black man, woman, and child of his/her rightful sense of self-identity – how they viewed themselves. The whites had to convince the slaves that they weren't human beings; they were "niggers." Since skin color was a permanent and easily recognizable difference between Africans and Europeans, it became the factor that was used to justify slavery ("blacks aren't fully human") and to make blacks feel bad about themselves.

Stage Two: *Enslavement and Psychological Domination*

The second stage in the development of the lie about black inferiority was slavery itself. For slavery to be sustainable, the slave traders and slave owners had to enslave not just the bodies of black people, but also their minds. They erased, destroyed and prohibited all vestiges of the slaves' African cultures – their languages, customs, rituals, religions, beliefs, foods, dress and celebrations. Slaves who came from Africa had no way to assert the identities they'd cherished as free people. In slavery, the once-proud tribal people were reduced to subhuman status, equal in value to a mule. Within a generation of coming to this hellish New World, African slaves' heritage was lost to them, and of course to their children as well.

Stage Three: *Destruction of Self-Concept*

Demoted from human to subhuman, the "nigger" was born. The third stage of the development of the belief in black inferiority was the transformation from human being to "nigger," which destroyed each slave's fundamental self-concept. It's here that the white man's lie about black inferiority began to creep into the black slave's psyche. Self-concept is the way we relate to ourselves: our fundamental sense of self-esteem, self-worth, self-confidence, self-evaluation and our ability to trust, among other things. All of these crucial pieces of psychological well-being were severely impaired by the imposition of the new "nigger" identity because black slaves began to believe they really were niggers.

It's hard to imagine how a person could be convinced that he or she is less than a full human being. But bombarded constantly with evidence of their powerlessness and lack of respect by whites, the black slave's self-concept eroded.

"Why me?" the new slave wondered. "Maybe I deserve to be treated this way."

Stage Four: *Internalizing the Lie*

Anyone experiencing powerlessness in the face of this kind of extreme adversity would eventually succumb to self-doubts. It is in the fourth stage that we began to perceive ourselves as inferior. We internalized – allowed into our hearts, minds and spirits – the lie of black inferiority.

What happened when we internalized the lie? All the personal measures of identity that were based on what the black slaves valued about themselves – the fact that they were "mother," or "man," or "leader," or "wise person," for example – receded into the background. As they struggled for day-to-day survival, not only did their self-concept suffer, but so did their range of emotions about what was happening to them. In the midst of the trauma of being enslaved and being treated as a "nigger" and expected to act like a "nigger" slave, those individuals were not able to respond to their situation authentically. It was not safe, for example, to be angry or to grieve openly, or even in private (if the slaves were even allowed privacy). This restriction on their expression of emotions was a problem for them psychologically and spiritually. It meant they weren't able to heal from the abuse they were experiencing and re-experiencing every day. Survival required capitulating to the masters' demands, so the slaves' true emotions went underground. Instead, self-blame, self-doubt and fear forced them to adapt behind masks they wore to survive in the hostile environment of slavery.

There were primarily three ways that slaves adapted to internalized black inferiority; they became master-identified, master-resistant or master-submissive. Today, we can understand master-identified black individuals as being preoccupied with white acceptance and standing apart from other blacks because they don't want to be associated with "nigger." My client Joe from Chapter One fits this definition. Master-resistant individuals reject everything white and are obsessed with who is and is not a credible or worthy black. Master-submissive individuals accept the "nigger" role, focusing on making it bigger and badder.

Master-submissive is really a paradox. The young people who glorify the "nigger" see themselves as resisting society's effort to define them, but they do it paradoxically by taking on the "nigger" role and exaggerating it. It seems to those of us on the outside that they are doing exactly what the myth of black inferiority expects of them, but it doesn't feel like that to these young people. I saw this firsthand when my nephew adopted a master-submissive race stance. "G," as he was called by his friends when he wasn't called "Nigga," stood on the corner, showing his underwear, using poor English, playing loud music and playing craps with his friends when he should have been in school or working. I even tried to bribe him to go to school with the promise of a car. But no, he wasn't going to play the white man's game like me. Even now, it hurts to remember because I was in love with this beautiful, brilliant boy from the moment he was born. I had dreams of him going to Harvard, not Howard (where I had gone – a sure sign of my own black shadow). But instead of nurturing his intelligence and his talents, Gary embraced the master-submissive race stance until it inevitably ended where the "nigger story typically does: prison.

Stage Five: *Adopting a Stance Toward Race*

The fifth stage in the development of the myth of black inferiority was developing a stance toward race as a way to control our anxiety. Feelings of inferiority were hidden from view by anti-black, pro-black or "baddest nigger" masks. As you probably figured out, contemporary blacks still adopt these various stances toward race. Does this sound familiar? "Race doesn't matter!" "It's always about race!" "You can't trust whites!" "You can't trust blacks!" "Black English is legitimate." "Black English is ridiculous." "You're one of us." "You're not one of us."

Here's my point: regardless of what stance you take, it is a reflection of your internalization of the myth of black inferiority. Believing in the myth of black inferiority, we become blame-oriented and driven to find flaws in blacks, including ourselves. All of these stances contribute to negative thinking that imposes limits on the black individual and the black group. Our tolerance for human imperfections at both the individual and group levels becomes stressed, as do our feelings of compassion and kindness toward one another.

Stage Six: *Self-Hate and Blaming the Victim*

In the sixth stage of the development of the myth of black inferiority, the individual is recruited into being self-hating by the alienating experiences of feeling personally flawed and blaming the victim – themselves. I saw this clearly in my 45-year-old client James. At the impressionable age of 10, James's fifth-grade white teacher stood him in front of his 99% white classroom after he did poorly on a test and said, "See James? He is never going to be anything." James was humiliated and unable to defend himself so he began to worry excessively about not being smart enough. His preoccupation with being smart and amounting to something led him to study obsessively, and compulsively go over homework to be sure he had done it correctly. James did not want to be just another dumb "nigger." These behaviors were the beginning of his later diagnosed obsessive compulsive disorder (OCD).

Flash forward years later, James, despite his doctorate degree, still obsessively checked things at work and greatly worried that he would miss something. He spent his weekends absorbed in work so he could stay ahead of deadlines and was miserably depressed. Although he saw a white psychiatrist for his OCD and depression, he came to see me so he could talk about how he didn't feel like a real man in his black skin. He felt ashamed of being black every time he saw homeless black men on the street begging for money. His own self-hatred and secret belief that he was somehow inherently flawed because he was black had oppressed him for many years. It took incredible courage for him to seek me out to talk about his negative feelings about being black, and over time he came to see how those feelings had ruled his life. It was a major step toward facing his black shadow and taking back the joy in his being.

Stage Seven: *Acting Out of the Myth of Black Inferiority*

We hurt ourselves with the lash of learned black inferiority each time we take one of the master-related stances toward race: when we withdraw from blacks, badmouth blacks, or blame everything in our lives on being black. When we allow self-hate to creep into our psyches, we are ultimately accepting the lie about the innate and irreparable inferiority of blacks. The seventh stage of the development of the myth of black inferiority takes it to a new level of tragic: we black people buy into the myth. We believe the lie!

We already know what happens when we reach Stage Seven: we act out on ourselves and other black people. For example, a black woman who operates a private catering service complained to me, saying, "Black people don't understand business." This woman's business was not going as well as she'd hoped. She then added, "I'm thinking about giving everything up and working for someone else." (Someone white, I assumed, although she didn't say it.) She blamed her black employees for driving away business, but because of her internalized black inferiority, she also secretly believed that she didn't understand business well enough to be a success. She saw her only option as giving up on her dream. Afraid of being revealed as the "niggers" we're so sure we are, we worry excessively about our own and others' blackness. The toxic nature of black relationships, work or personal, speaks to our unresolved slave trauma and the black shadow pulling our strings like marionettes.

We shouldn't blame ourselves for what slavery and racism have done to us. Our African ancestors were happy and whole human beings before they were kidnapped and forced into slavery, and they were incredibly strong to have survived and adapted in extreme conditions. In fact, we have two important pieces of knowledge to add to those missing branches of our family trees, and from which we can begin to build our own healing temple: our people were enterprising, and they were resilient.

History Lessons

History has played a monumental role in the myth of black inferiority. White America carefully and methodically restricted our access to institutions and information that would give us a real and continuous sense of our intelligence, purposefulness and enterprising natures. We continue to be fed a steady diet of negative images of black images, from Toms, Coons, servants, tragic mulattoes, Mammies, and bucks, to super-bad niggas, super-mamas, dope addicts, gangstas, sluts, pimps and criminals. This is yet another way the myth of black inferiority is reinforced and renewed for new generations of blacks and everyone else. Psychologically, what do these images of black people do to us? They leave us feeling silenced and incapacitated instead of energized. In short, we become victims.

It suits the black shadow to let us believe we are victims because it means we have no energy to defy or contradict the white story of racial superiority. More importantly, we don't credit ourselves with having the positive qualities needed to overcome the negative consequences of slavery. In this way, we stay non-threatening to whites. Shamed and humiliated by racist messages that white is the human ideal and therefore we should strive to be more like whites, we lose sight of what's really important: our relationships, our families, our ability to be healthy in mind, body and spirit and to raise healthy, happy children who know they are loved and capable of anything. As victims, our story is the opposite of this. Our community members struggle with fractured families. Too many of our children are raised by strangers in foster care. We have society's highest rates of addiction, poverty, unemployment, domestic violence and gang violence. Our young people suffer from high mortality rates, low graduation rates, and more. If you still doubt that the legacy of slavery and the myth of black inferiority are relevant in your life, then you, my friend, are in deep denial. The white lie still has a stranglehold on us.

Challenging Our Stance Toward Race

Black inferiority is an unconscious state of mind. You don't wake up in the morning and think, "I'm not as good as my white neighbor." But as we act out of the black shame that we inherited and absorbed from birth, we engage in self-defeating behaviors. We also judge and harm one another without consciously acknowledging that our black shadows make us reject ourselves and other blacks.

Like our slave ancestors, we've each had to develop our stance toward race – master-identified, master-submissive or master-resistant – and a range of coping mechanisms for daily life. Unfortunately, many of those coping skills that seem to be positive are still rooted in the myth of black inferiority. Today's modern-day stances toward blackness fall under three labels: "exceptional" blacks who succeed in a white world in spite of their racial disadvantage; "super-bad niggas," such as rappers and gang bangers, who make a career out of being everything white society fears; and militant blacks like Louis Farrakhan who reject white society and want to live in a black-only world. Of course, there are many more ways to be black, but these can seem like the only choices we have for being black people in America.

"Exceptional" Blacks and Soul Congruity

Have lighter skin, a middle-class upbringing and/or succeeding in school are some of the reasons "exceptional" blacks do better than the rest of their black peers. "Exceptional" blacks strive to be just as good as white folks, if not better. However, anxious to differentiate from those other blacks ("niggers"), they have a tendency to over-identify with whites, which naturally results in denial of their own black self-worth. Just as some Jews used assimilation to survive in anti-Semitic Europe before World War II, and changed their names to WASP-sounding ones to try to avoid anti-Semitism in America, "exceptional" blacks distance themselves from black culture and community to try to avoid the taint of blackness and prove that they are "just like" whites. (Some lighter-skinned brothers and sisters even pass as whites, and those who do find it very stressful to associate with black relatives and friends.) By implication, they're saying to themselves and the rest of the world that they are better than other blacks because they are more like whites.

"Exceptional" blacks struggle to make it in corporate and professional America, but it's an endless proving ground where everyone is expected to act white. And even success in that arena doesn't guarantee acceptance by the white corporate culture. It's an exhausting path for black people (and doubly so for black women, who also have to contend with corporate culture's sexism). Disconnected from their roots and not ever fully accepted by white culture, "exceptional" blacks can never achieve wholeness. Nowhere feels like home for them. Without wholeness, they have no chance at experiencing genuine self-acceptance. And self-love won't grow where there is no self-acceptance.

Autumn, a thirty-something professional black woman lived primarily in a white world with her white husband. She denied the existence of racism by reciting the many opportunities available to blacks if only *"they"* would take advantage of them. Whenever her black colleagues spoke of racism in the workplace, she quickly withdrew. After years of getting by this way, denying that racism was real, Autumn began to feel restless, anxious and dissatisfied with her life.

As her mother used to tell Autumn, "You can get by, but you won't get away." She had been, as she told me, "acting white but feeling black," and as she approached mid-life, she was questioning the meaning and purpose of her life. I often see "exceptional" blacks when they reach mid-life, because developmentally that's a time when we take stock of our lives and re-examine our choices. For professional blacks like Autumn who followed the white rules and achieved a modicum of success, they realized they weren't happy. "Success is a feeling that, without soul, you just don't have," she told me.

I've heard this realization referred to as "the nigger wake-up call." (In my new resolve not to use the N-word, I suggest we call it the "black wake-up call.") In search of the soul-man or soul-woman left behind, many a professional black has run back to the black church and community seeking self-healing and self-validation. Racial self-acceptance and reaffirming one's blackness is the antidote to years of walking around in white-face – the price of being a "qualified minority" at the mountain top of corporate America. Others gladly hand in their corporate/professional club card for jobs or careers that liberate them from the high price of downplaying their blackness. In the final analysis, soul congruity (awareness, expression, and acceptance of one's blackness) is what is necessary for mental and physical well-being.

Autumn had strayed so far from her roots that she wasn't in touch with her black self at all. She felt betrayed by the dominant culture's myth of the melting pot. She had done all the right things: she was well-educated, articulate, married to a white man and living in the suburbs with the right kind of white people. She was also angry, but anger was an emotion that was difficult for her to claim. Angry, she was another "angry black woman" and that made her feel too much like a "nigger."

I gave Autumn a cognitive life raft by teaching her to recognize her black shadow and understand how deeply the myth of black inferiority had been internalized in her body, mind and soul. In a racist society, she was a black object to be hated, and so she had learned to hate herself for being black. I appealed to her intellect, inviting her to explore the traumatic effects of racism on her own and other African Americans' psyches. Autumn had been thinking and acting the way she thought she was supposed to as an "exceptional" black, but she began to see how those denials of her black culture and heritage masked her shame at being black. Black shame comes from nursing the negative images and negative stereotypes that we are fed until they become integrated into our psyches, creating a reality of inferiority that then makes us feel guilty for not being smarter, prettier, and cleaner – code for "whiter."

It's the combination of the shame and fear of blackness that destroys our self-concept. That's another poisonous tentacle of the black shadow keeping us chained to self-hate. Autumn was hurting too much to continue dismissing racism by saying, "Black people blame race for everything." The strong wind of racism that whipped across her life while she was in the process of a tenure review at her university became a sudden storm. Her previously denied feelings of being treated like a second-class colleague whose work was taken less seriously than her white colleagues finally gathered enough raw force to produce Hurricane Autumn.

Autumn began to read more about racism and discovered the voices of other "exceptional" blacks who had gone through the same thing she was going through. She read me a passage from the book *Volunteer Slavery* by Jill Nelson: "My job. I feel like it's a daily assault on my integrity, my sense of self, who I am. Every day I have to justify myself, my ideas, the people I write about, to a bunch of people who don't care – a bunch of white folks who assume they're superior solely on the basis of their skin color."

Autumn told me, "I'm leaving the white-rigged workplace and going into private practice!"

Super-Bad Super-Niggas Living Up to Low Expectations

"You say I'm bad? I'll show you just how bad I am!" That's the super-bad "nigga's" mantra. Super-bad blacks over-idealize – glorify – the character of "nigger." Their socially unacceptable "nigger" actions such as being loud, dressing with jeans hanging off the butt, speaking poor English, looking menacing and so on, become both a source of personal power and a threat to society. Inflation of demonized aspects of "nigger" behavior creates a subculture of isolation where there is little or no awareness that the "nigger" stereotypes have become their self-fulfilling prophecies. Like my nephew, these black people tend to act in ways consistent with society's negative stereotypes of them: low-achieving, no ambition, embracing the roles of good-for-nothing bucks and welfare queens. Because society tells them that they are bad, they act bad. Setting up a negative expectation creates a negative outcome in the same way a positive expectation can lead to good grades and excellent work performance. If you believe you're bad, you will try to prove you're bad without consciously understanding that you're acting out of others' low expectations of you.

Living in their ghetto-fabulous world, it's all about claiming their power with the provocative persona of "nigger." Saying loudly, "I'm here. Deal with me," they might feel like they're challenging the myth of black inferiority. But because they don't understand their own black shadows, they don't understand that they are perpetuating the root of their pain. They can't heal; they can only self-destruct.

Rappers Tupac Shakur and The Notorious B.I.G. were two super-bad black icons. They flaunted their raunchy reputations and rapped a glamorous, but painful, reality of being black in poor, urban America. Niggatude ("I'm a nigga and proud of it") is just another strategy for surviving in a racist world, but the cost is high. Like He Lion of the folk tale, pride only gets them killed. And if they do survive, they need to ask why they're proud of being a "nigger." Isn't it the ultimate victory for the white lie when blacks themselves perpetuate the nigger stereotype and even claim it for themselves?

Calvin was a 16-year-old bad-ass with a bad attitude referred to therapy by the courts after attempting to fly off a New York subway platform. The psychiatrist who referred him thought it was a drug-induced psychosis, and also diagnosed a personality disorder. I was working in my first job at a community mental health center in East New York, and to be honest, Calvin scared me. He was just like the young black men hanging on the corner yelling out lewd comments as I walked the few blocks from the subway to work. He took full advantage of my fear, arriving early for his sessions and sitting in the waiting room looking hard-core and menacing as I walked by.

Therapy didn't go well. Calvin's mother showed up only for the first session because it was court mandated. She made it clear that she had other children to worry about and couldn't spend her time coming to therapy with Calvin. In subsequent sessions, Calvin refused to answer most of my questions. Instead, he told me stories to scare me, like how he beat someone up because of the way that person looked at him. When I tried to get him to talk about his emotions, he just looked at me with contempt. Thinking back, it was probably a mirror of the contempt he felt coming from me. I was seeing him the way the rest of society saw him: another low-expectation-having nigger, although I never said it aloud.

One day, Calvin told me he had a gun in his pocket. I felt a flash of panic. I should have immediately left the room and called the guard, but I was young (and foolish) and fairly certain he was bluffing and only trying to scare me. I stayed outwardly calm and confronted him about his bad-ass nigger persona. Calvin was taken aback by my apparent lack of fear. He actually thought about my question. That was the turning point in his therapy. The next session, he was willing to answer my questions and engage in therapy. What I realized is that Calvin needed to know that he could trust me and that I wouldn't just dismiss him as another hopeless black adolescent with a bad attitude.

As I got to know the real Calvin, I came to see that his alleged personality disorder was really his black shadow. He had experienced many losses in his young life, including an absent father and a mother who didn't have time for him because she was the single parent of six children. The housing project where he lived was a place of daily violence. Being a bad-ass nigger was a way to survive. It was a way to mask his fear and desperation by scaring the world away. But Niggatude as a strategy for happiness fails every time because it doesn't allow for authentic connection. Calvin expressed to me his constant feeling of disconnection and loneliness, even with his friends. He confessed that he'd started doing drugs because he felt so hopeless. His black shadow told him he would never amount to anything, never get out of the projects, and never be seen as anything but a good-for-nothing "nigger."

Calvin began to feel connected to me and even asked me to go out with him! I told him that it would not be appropriate for me to go out with him, but talked to him about establishing positive friendships with boys and girls his age. Calvin began to do better in school after a year of being in therapy and there were no more drug-induced incidents. Calvin is still special to me for what he taught me about myself and my own black shadow, even though I had not yet named it. By experiencing an authentic connection with me in therapy, Calvin lost his need to cling to his Niggatude. He was able to believe in his own humanity and develop self-worth and self-love.

Militant Blacks

Militant blacks claim to be the rightful owners of blackness. They pass judgment on who is a "good" race man or race woman based on a very narrow definition of what it means to be black. Black is defined in reaction to white and usually means the opposite of how whites act and what they like. For example, another one of my nephews was accused many times of not being a "real" black because he didn't listen to black music; he preferred classical music. At his historically black university, he was an outcast among his pro-black classmates.

Any black person who falls short of the Militant Blacks' strict code is summarily dismissed as an illegitimate black person. This kind of "us-them" attitude compounds the already troubling and hurtful divisions in the black community and serves to strengthen the black shadow by turning our energies against one another rather than against racism itself.

Learned black inferiority has many guises. Some of us hide our black shame and feelings of inferiority by appearing holier than thou in our blackness, setting ourselves up as the authority to judge who is black and who is not. The false self is gratified by the illusion of being superior; it's a protective shield against feeling inferior as a black person in society. It might seem as if one is outwitting the black shadow by reversing the message of black inferiority to say, "Black is the only good, and everything else is bad." But it's actually the other side of the same coin, and it causes its own problems for black people.

I've found that there's a little piece of each of these race stances in me. My "militant" side became apparent to me one day when I watched the reunion of talk show superstar Oprah Winfrey and relationship expert Iyanla Vanzant. Like many other blacks, I had always assumed that Oprah had thrown Iyanla under the bus when she chose to make a star of white psychologist Dr. Phil McGraw instead of promoting Iyanla. In my heart of hearts, I'd been disappointed in Oprah, to the extent that I privately judged her as not being "black enough." I wanted her to prove her blackness by choosing the black woman over the white man. My logical mind thought, "Whites take care of whites, and now Oprah is helping a white man when she could be helping a black woman!"

Listening to Oprah and Iyanla talk about their split on national TV, I heard Iyanla reveal that she was the one who'd decided to leave because she didn't trust Oprah's promise to help her launch her own show later. I was shocked. I, and a whole lot of other blacks, had been wrong in our assumptions and judgments about Oprah. I was grateful for this moment because it helped me look squarely at my own black shadow. I hope Oprah will forgive me for thinking less of her, and if I ever have the honor of meeting her, I will ask her forgiveness in person.

Like in the above example, behavior can be the measurement we use to determine whether someone is a "real" black or not when we're in a militant black mindset. But skin tone is very often another factor that makes us judgmental. Jon, a tall, handsome, light-skinned client of mine was visibly upset as he related details of a recent conversation he'd had with a darker-skinned black colleague, William. The two started talking about race, and Jon saw this as a great opportunity to connect with William. Not long into the conversation, William launched into a lecture about racial purity and "real blacks" and told Jon that his "shit color" meant he wasn't a real black man. Only dark-skinned African Americans were true black people. Light-skinned African Americans were damaged goods, the weak links in our race.

Discounted and devalued, an angry Jon counterattacked: "You ain't no real black man yourself. What black man would dis another black man?" Yet this is exactly what each of them did, exposing skin color as our covert measure for determining a black person's worth. Malcolm X, himself a light-skinned man who died for the cause of all black people's equality, would have turned over in his grave a few times if he heard this conversation.

"To express the various levels of contempt for various degrees of color, a vocabulary of self-hatred has been generated among African Americans," writes David K. Shipler in *A Country of Strangers*. "It includes 'rusty,' 'blueblack,' 'high yellow,' and a nasty little chant that darker children sometimes aim at lighter playmates: 'Light, bright, almost white! Light, bright, almost white!' "

Jerlene, a 43-year-old mother of five and grandmother of six, grew up in a family where it was common to express contempt for family members based on skin tone. She told me, "I don't want my grandson growing up feeling bad because he's darker than his brother." Jerlene's own grandmother had treated her lighter-skinned "grands" better than her darker ones. "My four-year-old Louie says he wants to be light," Jerlene explained. "So when he asked me if I was going to like his baby brother better because he was light, I said 'No!' I said, 'You don't want to be light. That's a shit color.' And Louie said, 'My brother has that shit color, right Grandma?' And I said, 'Right'."

Jerlene believed she was nothing like that grandmother because she wasn't favoring the lighter grandson. She wanted to be an ally to her darker-skinned grandson, but in doing so she was perpetuating the same hurtful dynamic of rejecting a child because of his skin color rather than valuing and loving each child in the family equally. When she came for therapy, we talked about a different conversation she could have with Louie to help him understand that he and his brother were both beautiful and equally loved by their grandmother, no matter what their color. We talked about how she might explain to Louie that she had made a mistake when she told him that his brother had "that shit color," and express her sorrow that she'd said something hurtful. She could explain that it was wrong to say that about another person, and hope that Louie would understand that he and his brother were both African American and we come in different colors. I suggested she and Louie go to the bookstore so she could find age-appropriate books to help foster positive self-esteem for black children. Jerlene discovered that helping Louie navigate these confusing waters of skin tone, blackness and envy also helped her to expose and challenge her black shadow.

We are caught up in the white culture's paradigm when we discriminate on the basis of skin color – privileging light or dark. In the '70s, our rallying cries of "Black Power" and "Black Is Beautiful" were still reactions to internalized ideas about black inferiority. We were supposed to take pride in ourselves *because* we were black, but simply reversing the paradigm doesn't fix the problem. We might have gained a temporary sense of positive black identity, but we still live in a racist society and the black shadow still plagues us, despite the slogans.

We must stop alienating one another on the basis of our skin color! Our race styles and attitudes drive wedges between us, and not only do we compromise our collective power and focus attention away from the real enemy – racism – but we cause pain and suffering to our own.

The Price of Learned Black Inferiority

I worry about all of us when it comes to the fallout of learned black inferiority, but I worry most of all about our young people. The signs are all there for us to see: it's taking a terrible toll on our sons and daughters, our nieces and nephews, our grandchildren. The group with the highest increase in the rate of suicide in the United States is young black males. Young black women are being incarcerated in rapidly increasing numbers for nonviolent, drug-related offenses. And black males already comprise the largest percentage of male inmates. (It must be said that many black male and female offenders have been imprisoned on nonviolent, drug-related offenses as a result of America's so-called War on Drugs, which was aimed primarily at poor and minority drug offenders.) Not only is this a tragedy for the men and women who are incarcerated, but we can't even wrap our minds around the extent of the collateral damage done to black families and communities whose loved ones are behind bars.

In *The New Jim Crow: Mass Incarceration in the Age of Colorblindness*, author Michelle Alexander makes a powerful case about the U.S. criminal justice system's role in marketing and enforcing black inferiority. She writes, "The limits of your ambition were, thus, expected to be set forever. You were born into a society that spelled out with brutal clarity, and in as many ways as possible, that you were a worthless human being. You were not expected to aspire to excellence: you were expected to make peace with mediocrity."

The mass incarceration of blacks reinforces the lie about black inferiority in the American imagination, and this time black people must fight against the scariest form of the lie of "nigger": the dangerous, white-woman-raping, violent black man. It's no wonder that the "felon" label makes it legal to discriminate against blacks in all the ways that Jim Crow laws discriminated against us based on race. In the new Jim Crow era, "felon" replaces "race," with all the tragic consequences.

Overcoming the Myth of Black Inferiority to Heal

Speaking about the myth of black inferiority opens a path for us to create a new and different story, one that empowers rather than weakens us as black and multiracial people. Before we can heal, we must first understand what the myth of black inferiority has done to us and how it continues to be perpetrated on black psyches. After we name the problem, we need to rewire our own psyches. By that I mean we consciously need to de-color-code our thoughts, feelings and behaviors. Do you know what your preferred race style is? Can you understand how it's working against you? Can you see another way to live free of the myth of black inferiority? The black shadow clings to it; it needs it! But by externalizing rather than internalizing black inferiority; by becoming an expert on its twists and turns through conversations with your family and friends and co-workers; by sharing your insights with others about how it affects your life, what it talks you into doing or not doing, and how it sets you up to interact with other blacks, you can separate your true self from the false self created through black shame. Personal power will come to you through this process of acknowledgement and testifying.

For many years, my scholarly work focused on the effects of external racism on couples and families. But the more I dug into the myth of black inferiority, the more I came to see how important it was to examine intra-black family racism. I knew I would come up against resistance from my black colleagues, because I was "airing the dirty laundry" not only in our community, but to the white community. I presented workshops, gave lectures and wrote about skintone privilege in black families, which made me confront my own, ingrained ideas about beauty and color. At the same time, I began to challenge the use of "nigger" in my family. I used my ideas and writing to open conversation in my family. I didn't take it personally when I met with resistance. The one thing I know as a therapist is that change is a journey and not a straight line. Also, I know that each person has his or her own path and that we're each unique.

In my family, everybody knows that I am not the most patient person. When I see a problem, I want to fix it. I want results to come quickly, but exposing and eradicating the black shadow is deep, gut-busting work for the soul. It requires compassion and encouragement, and it takes time. There's no sudden "satori" experience. Knowing this, I resolved to be understanding, forgiving and compassionate with myself and other blacks, and I reminded myself of this promise when I would feel short of patience. Remembering that I still have intrusive thoughts about black inferiority – even after years of examining its impact on me personally, my family and our larger community – helps me to be understanding and cut others more slack as they struggle to get free of their black shadows.

The black shadow is familiar territory. It's been with us our whole lives. Most of us stick to what's familiar from inertia, fear, or lack of something better to replace it. I believe doing something different is a choice, but we need options. Black shadow awareness is about seeing those other options so we can make different choices.

We can't wait for anyone else to do this work for us. An apology from white America will do little to reverse the tremendous psychological damage done to our ancestors and to us by slavery. The only way to heal is for each individual black person to challenge the myth of black inferiority and get out from under its heavy weight. Free of the victim role, we could live and let other blacks live by their own standards without the fear of being judged a "nigger."

We may always live in a racist world. But the myth of black inferiority doesn't have to be a fixed state in black America. Confronting uncontested myths of black people's inferiority will help us to develop new thinking, replacing the unconscious mental image we have of a black person as a "nigger."

Internalized black inferiority is likely the reason African Americans tweeted negative comments about Olympic gold-medal gymnast Gabby Douglas's hair when she made history at the 2012 Olympics. Instead of taking pride in this young black woman's incredible achievement, her own people made snarky comments about her appearance. If we look at those comments through the lens of the black shadow, it's clear that our concern about skin color and hair comes directly from the centuries of enslavement we endured in this country. We viewed her as we imagined a racist white audience would see her: a black girl with messy ("too kinky") hair. We have taken those racist beliefs inside us. We police ourselves and one another. Gabby Douglas was representing not only the United States, but all black Americans. Policing one another was a mechanism for survival during the centuries of slavery. If one slave got out of line, all the slaves might feel the lash, or worse. And even though slavery is over, we still perpetuate the lessons we learned as slaves and pass them on to the next generation. This is just one small example of the truth that slavery is not irrelevant to contemporary African Americans.

Psychiatrist Alvin F. Poussaint and co-author Amy Alexander described the physical and psychological toll that racism has taken on blacks as "posttraumatic slavery syndrome" in their book, *Lay My Burden Down*. People who have been traumatized often try to cope by avoiding exposure to reminders of that experience. They tend to be on edge, uptight about the trauma happening again. Therefore, it is not uncommon for blacks to be obsessed with how we and other blacks talk, look and act because we were enslaved and then discriminated against for having black skin.

Imagine a future generation of African Americans desensitized to "nigger." Undoubtedly, we would have greater self-acceptance and we wouldn't have need to gather in hushed circles in the home, workplace, and community to tell "nigger-shit" tales that say as much about the black teller's self-image as they do about the main "nigger" character in the story.

We've all heard numerous times from each other that you can't trust blacks to do competent work. How many of us nay-sayers have actually tried to understand the origin

of this attitude? How many of us would even think to connect it to the myth of black inferiority that now causes us instinctively to accept that blacks are intellectually inferior and incompetent? How else do you explain concluding that you can't trust all black people after one bad experience? And why is it that you don't rule out hiring white service providers or white professionals as a group after one of them screws up? How many blacks who confirm society's view of us as lazy, shiftless, and unreliable have an inkling that the myth of black inferiority is the program that they have refused to challenge? Why else would you expect black employers to excuse your poor performance? And why else would you set such a low standard for yourself?

Distance is created between the nay-sayers and those who fit the black stereotypes. Each projects his or her internalized black inferiority onto the other. But nothing is done to alter the unconscious "nigger" image at the heart of their projections. Consequently, no learning occurs for black people to challenge racial distortions of themselves.

This became a topic of conversation during a focus group I ran on the black shadow. We were talking about how we're habitually silent about slavery, even though black people were the innocent victims. "There's a tremendous amount of societal pressure and black support for minimizing the effects of slavery," said Nia, a 34-year-old participant. "When you attempt to bring it out, you're automatically and quickly squashed with, 'Oh, those things are over,' or 'We don't do that in our house.' It's like this constant battle within and without black America that helps to perpetuate the problems. They'll talk every now and then about monetary reparations for what was taken from us during slavery. But nobody talks about the kind of psychic reparations we need inside to really heal from all the incredible destruction."

Even the sea gives up its secrets after sheltering them for ages. Breaking our silence and finally talking about our people's history of slavery will lead African Americans to a more promising future because we'll finally be able to heal from its toxic effects on our lives. We'll finally be able to demystify and then vanquish the black shadow. It's up to us. We have the power and it's our choice to resist the forces that want to keep us down, keep us believing we're inferior because we're black. As a community, we can collectively reframe our identity, resist racism and challenge the myth of black inferiority.

The slaves expressed their desire for freedom in the black folk tales we inherited. Black folk tales remind us of our ancestors' resistance and resilience. *The People Could Fly: American Black Folktales told by Virginia Hamilton* tells a tale of field slaves who simply stopped working one day, lifted their arms and flew away. In black folklore, there was talk of flying Africans, which likely was code for slaves disappearing or running away from slavery. Also, it may have been the slave's wish to rise above slavery to freedom. I like to think it honors the millions of slaves who never knew freedom and makes us remember their enduring wish for freedom.

We, too, must have an enduring wish to be free from the black shadow. With compassion and forgiveness, blacks can begin to develop relationships of mutual trust and respect with one another. We can create a non-toxic atmosphere where we can hold each other accountable without indicting the whole race when one individual misbehaves or exiling our brothers and sisters from the community with our negative judgments. With focus and commitment, we can manage, contain and prevent more unnecessary black suffering. Through connection, we can construct resistance and find an end to grief.

The Million Man March was a wondrous example of constructive resistance. Black men from every state in the union and from every walk of life forged a powerful connection and challenged the myth of the irresponsible black male when they came together in the nation's capitol. The sea of black faces that stared back at me from the television did not fit the description of black men penned by the larger society.

Slavery is America's birth defect, not blackness. Awake to the myth of black inferiority, we can speak out against it. Closer to home, we can refuse to promote the myth of black inferiority by not making "black" the butt of jokes. We can stop dividing ourselves out of black shame and self-hate. We can challenge our families, friends and colleagues when they thoughtlessly parrot society's myth of black inferiority. And then, finally, we can get to know our real history.

Exercises
A 7-Step Black Shadow Recovery Process

Start your own healing process right now using this 7-step recovery process.

Step 1: Remember and honor our history of slavery. Consciously engage in this practice of recognizing slavery's impact on the black community's collective psyche and on your own psyche.

Step 2: Acknowledge the black shadow in your own life. Become "shadow alert." Feelings of hopelessness, powerlessness, shame and rage; of not being smart enough, pretty enough, or worthwhile are opportunities for shadow sightings. Negative reactions to other blacks are also opportunities to name the shadow. Still other opportunities for meeting the shadow are found in language used to describe blacks, either-or thinking about blacks and whites and an unrealistic expectation of sameness for blacks.

Step 3: Identify your race stance and the masks you wear to survive under racism. For example, player, super-black woman, mainstream ("I'm a human being"), color blind, class, comparison ("I'm as good as any white person/I'll never be a white man/woman"), pro-black, bad black and anti-black. Understand what these masks mean to you and what they cost you to wear.

Step 4: Dialogue with your black shadow so it doesn't have the only word. Have internal conversations with it about your feelings/reactions that are rooted in being black. Think of the reasons you feel the way you do. Evaluate your feelings. If you had a magic wand, what would you change about yourself and your life? What would you replace them with?

Step 5: Challenge the myths of white superiority and black inferiority with historical knowledge. Get to know your black history. Break your silence. Talk with others about the black shadow. Stop the automatic "assumption of goodness" for whites and the automatic "assumption of badness" for blacks.

Step 6: Focus on self. When you focus on the other you can't change. Change can only occur when you focus on the self.

Step 7: Accept yourself! Make a personal commitment to the self to achieve self-mastery and self-confidence. Recognize, appreciate and accept personal and individual standards of blackness. Look at human imperfections as universal and understand that no group of people is all good or all bad. Develop basic self-respect and self-love, and a feeling of entitlement to equal human rights and a sense of empowerment when it comes to pursuing equal rights. Nurture your sense of purpose and shared interest in black group survival, but don't buy into the "all blacks are the same" lie from white or black America.

The Self-Rejection Quiz

Are you tuned in to self-rejection? Take this test to find out. When you can identify self-rejection, you can let go of the negative feelings and behaviors that rob you of the emotional, physical and spiritual energy needed to improve your life, which you need to be your best and highest self. Think about each of the statements below and choose the answer that comes closest to the way you think or feel, and keep track of your score as you go:

> **Never true = 1**
> **Rarely true = 2**
> **Sometimes true = 3**
> **Frequently true = 4**
> **Always true = 5**

1. I become agitated or angry when black people act up.

2. I feel depressed or frustrated when I'm next in line and the white (or black) salesperson overlooks me to help the white person behind me, but I don't say anything. Or I snap, getting aggressive.

3. I am embarrassed by or ashamed of black children running around in stores.

4. I intentionally act the part of "nigger" when whites (and blacks) regard me suspiciously.

5. I feel that I am constantly being judged because of the color of my skin.

6. I feel like whites do about some blacks.

7. I wish I weren't black or feel ashamed when watching or hearing

about stereotypical images of blacks in mixed company.

8. I don't feel I've been victimized by racism.

9. I don't feel comfortable around blacks who are not like me—my kind.

10. I hate working with blacks and it would be worse to have a black for a boss.

11. I pay special attention to what blacks are doing because it could make me look bad.

12. I would never hire a black person to work for me because you can count on them to screw up.

13. I don't feel connected to my siblings since they graduated from college or didn't go to college.

14. I avoid the old neighborhood because the blacks living there don't want anything out of life.

15. I check out a newborn's hair and skin color.

16. I call other black people racial names.

17. I won't date a dark/light man/woman.

18. I am very critical of my own and/or other blacks' looks and speech.

19. There's nothing beautiful about nappy hair.

20. I feel tormented and hopeless as a black person.

20-40 Points: You have low self-rejection. Share your positive self-esteem and group identity with other blacks. Become a big brother/big sister or mentor for children of inmates or other black children needing positive role models in their lives.

41-60 Points: You have moderate self-rejection. You are at-risk for not reaching your greatest potential. Fear and low self-esteem may hold you back. Look closely at your life to see what unconscious negative beliefs may be blocking your success.

61-100 Points: You have high self-rejection. Talk to a therapist who is culturally competent. Read self-help books. Consider finding support from a trusted friend, minister, counselor, teacher or family member to get in touch with your inner feelings.

Chapter 3
The Black Family: For Better and Worse

When an African American baby comes into the world, one of the first conversations the parents and extended family have as they gaze at the newborn is whether the child has "good" skin or "good" hair. Almost from the moment of birth, the parents and relatives of the child are caught up in a pattern of thinking and behaving toward that child in ways that reflect the internalization of the lie of black inferiority. The child's own family will carry the racist society's expectations. If he's light-skinned, he'll be celebrated as beautiful, smart, a future president. If she's dark-skinned, the prognosis for her future will not be that bright.

"My grandmother, who was very fair-skinned, treated my sisters better than me," remembered Barbara Ann, a 36-year-old client. "I was the dark one. I was blamed for everything. My three sisters got away with everything. I was seen as the sneaky one. I was laughed at, teased and called 'blackie' at home. I could never understand my grandmother's dislike of me. She would say hurtful things like, 'You're black and ashy,' or, 'You're going to end up pregnant and on welfare'."

As a family therapist who works with African American and multiracial families, I am constantly confronted with this most tragic aspect of the black shadow: we often treat our lighter-skinned children better than their darker-skinned siblings. That life lesson is never forgotten by either of the children. Even if the difference in shade is barely perceptible, everyone in the family – the children, especially – is well-aware of who is lighter, and that lighter-skinned child may be consciously or unconsciously treated with more love and kindness by parents and extended family members, teachers and people in the community. More may be expected of the lighter-skinned offspring, and more encouragement, emotional support and even financial support given to that child. When this occurs, the darker child feels the sting of rejection again and again, and grows sad, bitter, despondent, angry or depressed at the deep unfairness of the situation. The black shadow invades the most sacred bond between parent and child, and parents unwittingly become its agent by teaching their children, through their own behavior, that to be dark-skinned is to be inferior and therefore less worthy of love.

"I never thought about my own dark skin when my grandmother said negative things about dark-skinned blacks," Rochelle admitted in a near-whisper during a workshop I gave on racism in African American families. "I almost didn't marry my husband because she said he was too black. She still thinks it's cute to tell how she used to hit my father as a baby because he was so black and ugly. She didn't want anybody to see him. She says he was too black and ugly to be her baby. She was ashamed to be his mother. She treated him badly. Now all he does is work. He's always dressed in a suit and is always going back to school for something. My grandmother has a light-skin thing going on. She gives my light-skinned cousin all the consideration while not giving me any. And I've been afraid that she wouldn't like me if I said no to her. It had to have an impact on me growing up in a family with a grandmother who hated her son's dark skin, and with a father who wasn't comfortable with himself because he felt inferior. I learned, without knowing it, that I was less-than, too, because of my dark skin."

Even in families where society's racism is openly discussed, our internal family racism is very rarely named or challenged. Discussed or not, it's real and it's pervasive in the black and multiracial community. Our elders teach us through their words, actions and silences that dark skin is undesirable and light skin is valuable. We're raised on the lie of black inferiority and we witness the subtle and overt ways it creates power, alliances, cut-offs and friction within our own families. I see this manifestation of the black shadow over and over again in the African American and multiracial families I work with. I hear stories about it from my students and colleagues, from participants in workshops and focus groups, from my friends at church and in my neighborhood. And I witness it in my own family. If this book does only one thing, I wish it would help us change our hearts and minds so we can spare another generation of black children from experiencing the devastating pain of racism perpetrated by their own families.

Passing on the Black Shadow

Without being aware of it, parents are delivering their children into the hands of the black shadow every time they regard them through the lens of race – every time they measure and judge a child's worth based on their skin tone. When their parents judge them for being light or dark, it disturbs the black child's identity development process. Children are already bombarded with negative messages about dark skin color when they watch television, read books, go to school, shop at the mall, etc. To absorb these racist attitudes from their own parents is deeply bewildering for a young child. When black adults perpetuate the myth of black inferiority in their relationships with children, it has a traumatic impact on the child. Showing skin color preference in our families, we give children mixed messages about the connection between appearance and self-worth, which fosters insecurity and deep ambivalence about being dark. They naturally – and tragically – associate their entitlement to love and acceptance with their skin color.

To develop strong self-esteem and confidence, children need to feel valued and celebrated as unique individuals. If we teach them that skin color is a factor in our ability to value them, aren't we teaching them that the lie about black inferiority is true? Being rejected or privileged because of one's skin-tone is an experience nearly every single black or multiracial child has had, no matter how educated and successful his or her parents are, or how respected they are in the community.

I know what I'm saying here is deep, and I know that black people have a very hard time talking openly about this because it's so painful. I see the fallout of internal family racism in my therapy office all the time: couples who have problems because a husband or wife has never been able to feel lovable because of a family history of rejection based on skin tone; young men and women who sabotage their own dreams out of a sense of hopelessness and anger that they can never make their parents proud because they were born too dark. The myth of black inferiority is the foundation of our racist society, but it's also reinforced in our own families. The vast majority of us have internalized the lie of black inferiority, and because we're unaware of our black shadows we're passing it on to our children.

Lighter is Better

The problem isn't that black people are bad parents. We can't blame ourselves for unconsciously believing that lighter is better. We've been trained by every social message around us to understand that black is inferior to white. Some parents have said to me that they do wish their children had lighter skin because it's hard to be dark in a racist society. They are well-aware of the discrimination dark-skinned black people face, and they wish their children were somehow light enough to escape it.

"I feel my children are blessed to have light skin," 37-year-old Sydney told me frankly during a therapy session. We were discussing her feelings about her own dark skin. "I feel that way because I want them to have the advantages. I can remember things that happened because of the color of my skin. Maybe they won't go through that."

Many parents would agree with Sydney and see no reason not to be glad when their children are lighter than they are. "I think we all want our children to have the advantage of having an opportunity," she went on to tell me. "The opportunity seems to be that the lighter you are there's going to be more of an advantage for you somewhere out there. Now I have two children who are fairer than me. In fact, my little one is so much fairer that I felt like I was babysitting when she was born, to be honest. I said, 'Whose child is this?'" Sydney's wide smile described her delight about having a light-skinned baby.

When I asked her if she thought it was a good thing to focus so much attention on her children's skin tone rather than on their unique gifts and personalities, she was thoughtful. "I try to think how can I make the difference in them and let their light shine a little bit better than the skin, but their skin is going to make the first impression."

Sydney is right. The world will first judge her children by the shade of their skin. But I felt sad listening to her because racism is so embedded in our world view that we use it to judge our own babies. We have more hope for our lighter children, and therefore we create more advantages and opportunities for them than for their darker siblings and cousins. In some cases, we unconsciously give up on our darker children before they're even out of the crib.

The Dark Shadow Silence

The list of things black people haven't felt safe enough to talk about is long. We're only on Chapter 3, and we've already covered our reluctance to acknowledge our history of slavery and its residual effects on us, today. We've talked about the many ways the myth of black inferiority makes it hard for us to love and accept ourselves and thrive in the world. And now we have a third topic – internal family racism – that black families absolutely must discuss openly. A friend read an early draft of this manuscript and told me, "You're going to offend some people with this book!"

Please don't be offended. We need to talk about these issues in order to heal and be whole. Our silence only serves to let the black shadow grow stronger and plant its seeds in our children. By talking about it, we can stop the cycle and cut it off at the root.

We know we love our children, but the fact is that black mothers and fathers have internalized the myth of black inferiority. We are not aware that we have bought into the myth of black inferiority, so we unconsciously believe our darker-skinned children are less beautiful, capable, moral, ambitious, worthy and lovable than our lighter-skinned children. Generations of silence on this pattern of favoritism and rejection have normalized this pattern in African American families. Parents experienced the same pattern of favoritism and rejection in their families, and they pass it on.

Becoming a parent can bring up feelings of confusion and ambivalence toward darker children, which can spark more feelings of self-hate, anger, depression and a host of other negative emotions. I can't count the number of clients and workshop participants who have expressed regret and pain about how they were scorned by other black people – family members, neighbors, community members – for being too black, and how they went ahead and perpetuated that same dysfunctional behavior when they became adults.

"I didn't grow up around white folks," one woman told me during a workshop I gave on race in Philadelphia. "It was in my black neighborhood that I was called 'black' and 'ugly' because I was dark-skinned. I was called other names like 'ink spot' and 'ape.' Children laughed at me and said that I was dirty just because I was dark. Children refused to play with me and I often felt dirty and ashamed of myself no matter how much I bathed. I am 57 years old and I still feel the pain. I treated my children the same way. When they were small, I always scrubbed the darkest the hardest, trying to rub some of the black off. I used some of the same names on them that had been used on me. I didn't praise them or tell them they were pretty because I was taught that dark-skinned people were ugly. I didn't know any better. I never learned to love myself. And I didn't know how to love them or to teach them how to love themselves."

The damage done to us by the lie of black inferiority, by the lie of "nigger," is heartbreaking. But if we're mindful and alert to the black shadow's manipulations, we can stop ourselves from passing it on. We can make home and family and neighborhood a place where the black shadow can't get any traction. Future generations are counting on us to do this work, for their benefit and for our own. Confrontation, communication and cooperation can open wide the gates of freedom, expunging the hidden wounds of internalized black inferiority and creating space for the development of individual and family soul.

The Stealing of Soul

Our families set us up, for better and worse, for our lives as adults. Our ability to form mutually nurturing relationships, to trust, to forgive; and our parenting style and ability to express love and resolve conflict are all imprinted on us at a young age by our caregivers. Our misguided beliefs about the inferiority of blacks – deeply internalized in our unconscious minds – end up sentencing darker-skinned family members to live their adult lives waiting to be pardoned for being the wrong shade of black. Psychologically bankrupt, these individuals struggle with the feelings of rejection, shame, hopelessness and despair that formed during their earliest years. It affects their adult relationships, their friendships, their relationships with themselves and their relationships with their children.

Home was where they learned to despise themselves because they were born with dark skin. The black shadow stole their souls from a very early age. The capacity to love one's self and one's family is reduced when individuals and families lack "soul," by which I mean genuinely caring relationships based on each individual's unique gifts, personality, temperament, intelligence, kindness, spiritual capacity and essential Being. The soul of black families is poisoned by the black shadow's measuring stick of skin color, hair and education. We elevate the human qualities of those children and family members who are most white – least "nigger"; and we denigrate and despise those who are most black – most "nigger."

Why do we let the black shadow rule our lives? How can parents look at their baby and think, "ugly" because her skin is darker than theirs? We are ruled by the black shadow for two reasons: because we live without awareness that we've bought into the myth of black inferiority; and because we are still afraid of being branded "nigger." We instinctively distance ourselves from anything that will leave the stink of it on us, even rejecting our own children on a certain level.

Even the most loving parents are burdened by the pressure of society's stereotype of black people as being innately primitive, barbaric, untrustworthy and immoral. This lie of black inferiority creates a conflict in parents: they want to protect their children, but their children better not behave in ways that validate the stereotypes. These are the messages we give our kids: "Don't touch anything. Don't put your hands on things when you go into a store because people might think you're trying to steal something. Stop acting foolish! Black children are always acting up, making white folks think we're all a bunch of fools. Get your black behind over here. Do something with that nappy hair of yours."

Unmasking Segregation in our Families

Black families can't be soul-centered in the split state of light against dark and dark against light. We put on a good face for others, but in reality we're repressing our seething anger at the unfair treatment; we're wracked with jealousy, or sadness or shame. As we stratify along the lines of physical appearance and the myths and fantasies associated with white and black features, brothers and sisters harbor unspoken resentments toward one another that last a lifetime and are passed on to the next generation. They learn to hide their true selves rather than allowing themselves to trust others with their authentic being. As a therapist, I see the harm that this does every day. We choose self-containment and self-concealment over intimacy with our beloveds and the result is a level of loneliness and fear of rejection that never leaves us.

Racism keeps us segregated and separated from our own family members. If we can't be close to them, then whom can we ever trust? We already struggle to be accepted by a white-dominated, racist world, and now even our families aren't safe havens. Under the mask of "happy family," feelings of sadness and abandonment are staggering. We wonder who will ever cherish us and love us when we're the wrong color.

Complicated Judgments

African Americans, desiring to rise above the "inferior-because-black" stigma, end up unconsciously assigning various levels of social status to family members based on appearance (whiter) and achievement (educational, professional, financial). The favorite child is often seen as "perfect," which affects the self-development of all siblings, putting them at risk for not developing their potential. I know this firsthand, because in my family I was the favorite child. I was born to a dark-skinned mother who believed she was the ugly duckling. Her only sister was the beautiful swan because she was light-skinned. I was lighter in complexion than my mother, though not very fair. My father, however, was very fair with "good hair," and I sometimes think by association these characteristics were assigned to me. As a child, I remember being praised for my looks. I also remember everyone thinking that I was my light-skinned aunt's daughter. (Still today, some of those people think my aunt is my mother.) My mother jealously held me close when this would happen. She had a light (pretty) daughter who people thought couldn't belong to her because she was dark (ugly). Only my light aunt could be the mother of a pretty (light) daughter. And now my mother had something that her sister did not: me. To this day, my aunt says to me, "I wish you had been my daughter."

That same aunt has never once uttered these words to my sister, Brenda. Brenda was born four years later and was darker than I, with shorter hair. When we would go out walking with our mother as kids, grown people would tell my mother how cute I was while saying nothing about my sister.

Two things took shape in me from a very early age: I began to feel like my mother's trophy and my sister's protector. Very early on, I began campaigning for my sister to be valued. When she was 4 years old, I convinced my teacher to put her in the school play. Brenda was not in school yet, but I taught her a poem that she spoke at my school's Christmas Play. I wanted her to be seen and valued. I didn't want her to be left behind. It was never spoken aloud, but I knew it was skin color that made people choose me over her, and the unfairness of this made me feel bad. This was my little sister and she was beautiful to me.

CHAPTER 3 – THE BLACK FAMILY: FOR BETTER AND WORSE

My mother was smart and had dreams of going to college, but she dismissed those dreams because she felt ugly and therefore unworthy. But she and my father both let me know that those dreams were possible for me, and so I believed in myself and earned a Ph.D. and have had a very successful professional career. But all along, I was haunted by the truth that even though my sister Brenda is smarter than I am, only I was encouraged and expected to do well in life using my mind and my talents to their fullest. My parents didn't have faith in Brenda's abilities, so I tried to compensate. I encouraged Brenda and told her I believed in her, but she dropped out of high school. My brother, also darker than I, also dropped out. I recently asked Brenda about this and she said, "Mom probably didn't think we were too bright." She then added, "I still tell my friends that you and Mom didn't think I was competent to raise my own children so you came to get them a lot, and I said 'Good'."

It stung to hear her think the worst of me. I didn't tell her what was in my heart just then – that I had taken on the role of her protector long ago. Hearing my sister say that I thought she was incompetent was painful and I needed to get my emotions in check before talking more about this with her. I didn't want her to think I was defensive or dismissive of her feelings. Later, I shared with her how I felt growing up and told her that I understood how she might have misunderstood my help and taken it as a sign that I didn't believe in her. Brenda and I – like my mother and her sister – are close, but the black shadow is an uncomfortable undercurrent in our relationship, as it is in theirs.

Eventually, Brenda did finish high school and earned a college degree, and she even attended law school for a time. My sister believes that people do things when they're ready. My hope is that she and I are ready now to stop the black shadow from driving us apart, and that we're ready to stop it from being passed on to the next generation of our family.

Being the "perfect," favored child is a double-edged sword. I felt there was a lot resting on my shoulders, and it was hard to be an object of my parent's ambitions rather than an authentic, whole person who had fears and doubts. Sometimes I felt like I'd be exposed as an impostor. I knew it was the luck of the draw that I had the lightest skin among my siblings. I've seen in my clients who were assigned the role of favored child that some even come to believe that their success really is a direct result of their "superior" skin color. This false belief only leads eventually to confusion and self-hate as a black person.

Sometimes, the favorite child is groomed for the role of family savior, carrying the weight of the family's well-being on his/her shoulders. Family resources, including attentiveness, may be unevenly distributed to ensure that the favorite child-savior achieves success. African Americans have typically regarded the success of one family member as the success of the entire family. Historically, one member's success required the pooled efforts and financial resources of all family members. And for their sacrifices, payback was expected. "Never forget those who helped you to get where you are," and "Never forget your blood," are stamped into the savior's DNA. The savior's relationship to the family often becomes one of obligation, and the family's relationship to the savior is overshadowed by imposed expectation. Consequently, the individual soul of the savior may be compromised since s/he may feel disconnected from self, unable to pursue personal interests because of the perceived debt owed to the family. Saviors are expected to put the collective first and sacrifice personal needs and desires, which may lead to feeling devalued and taken for granted. And in most cases, the savior ends up feeling lonely and disconnected from family members, feeling valued only for what he or she gives rather than who he or she is.

"It was always me," 39-year-old Vanessa told me during a therapy session. "I was the pretty one, the smart one, the one who could fix things. No one ever thinks about *me*. What about *me*? I don't feel like a real member of the family. My brother and sister just seem to tolerate me. I'm not a part of their closed circle. I get called for favors. They don't bother to ask how I'm doing. They're always saying I was the favorite child. But Mom mothers them. Me – I mother Mom! I'm supposed to be 'lucky.' I'm a lawyer, married to a lawyer, and live in a big house. Still, I wish somebody could see me. I'm tired."

It's not a stretch to imagine the difficulties faced by the brothers and sisters who can never measure up to the idealized favorite child because they are too dark-skinned. Resentment, guilt and shame are typical responses to being the one left behind, the disappointment. The subtle or overt competition among siblings creates an emotional rift among family members. What results is a confusing mix of feelings: a sense of loyalty to the family along with self-preserving disengagement from the family.

Helping our children develop their full potential means that we must be honest about the presence of our own black shadows and internal family racism. If we don't challenge the myth of black inferiority that is at the core of internal family racism, we don't give our children their best odds for success and we pass on the black shadow to our children's children.

Years before my mother was diagnosed with Alzheimer's, she and my aunt made many disparaging comments about the light or white women they believed were making fools out of their sons and grandsons who were dating them. This became a perfect opening for challenging our own internal family racism. To lower their defenses, I reminded them of the stories they used to tell about how their own grandmother used to overtly favor their much lighter-skinned cousins. My mother and aunt were daughters of their grandmother's darkest daughter and therefore they were treated like second-class family members. While their lighter-skinned cousins were invited to eat specially prepared food at their grandmother's dining room table, my mother and her sister were sent to eat a plainer menu of foods in the kitchen.

Next, I talked to my aunt and my mother about their relationship to their mother. I knew that my aunt believed my grandmother was jealous of her because she had lighter skin. In fact, my aunt once said that my grandmother told her specifically that she chose to marry my grandfather instead of a "yellow" man because she didn't want "yellow" girls who would think they were better than her. Also, I knew my mother believed my grandmother favored my aunt because she was lighter.

By talking very personally about their pain and disappointment of being treated badly because of their skin tone, they started to talk honestly about skin color privilege in our family. My mother and aunt told all their children that we were beautiful, but even so, my siblings, cousins and I always knew that skin color mattered. When they spoke about other blacks, light skin denoted beauty and dark skin connoted ugly. I pointed out this contradiction to my mother and aunt and suggested that the adults could help the children in our family to have better self-esteem if we stopped making color valuations or using color to describe individual African Americans. I concluded with, "Maybe the future men in our family will be more concerned with love and respect than skin color."

I told my family members and I tell my clients that we have to remember that skin color preference was programmed into us over centuries and will not disappear overnight. We must consistently and persistently become mindful of our own attitudes and edit our own comments so that our children don't learn the sad lessons of racism from us. Fingerpointing and blaming are not the best strategy to start these conversations in the family. It's better to engage family members on the personal level – invite them to speak about what they've experienced and what they notice happens in the family around skin color privilege.

Dismantling the Black Shadow By Advocating for our Children

While we challenge racism in our own families, we also need to help children learn how to constructively challenge it in the outside world. The more we face our black shadows, the better we can see opportunities to prevent our children from learning that black is inferior. I remember when my niece Anique was nine years old, her private Quaker school studied a different culture each year as a way of teaching students to appreciate diversity. That year, African culture was chosen. The children watched films about Africa and learned about how masks play an important role in religious and cultural ceremonies. The children then made masks in their art classes. Right before Halloween, a letter was sent home telling all parents not to buy Halloween costumes because the children would be wearing the African masks that they had worked so hard on. That letter sparked a family discussion between the adults about the racial implications of wearing sacred masks on a day used for scaring and tricking people for candy. When asked how she felt, Anique stated clearly that she did not want to participate because the masks were worn in religious ceremonies and she thought it was disrespectful to the people of Africa.

Two decisions were made in the family meeting: Anique's feelings would be honored and validated; and the family's view that the school was being racially insensitive (no matter how well-intentioned) would be communicated to the principal. With my sister's permission, I served as family spokesperson. I asked for the job because I wanted to propose they create a board of cultural consultants to assist with such matters in the future. I was also willing to serve as a volunteer cultural consultant.

The principal was receptive to our feedback, but concerned about the other children who were looking forward to wearing their masks in the Halloween parade. I reiterated my family's belief that wearing the masks in the parade would risk reinforcing ingrained beliefs about Africans as scary monsters, and that this was disrespect, not appreciation, of Africa. The principal stated that she wanted to seek the advice of teachers and that she would get back to me.

In a second call, the principal informed me that the art teacher, who was Puerto Rican, defended the children's wearing of the masks on Halloween. The masks didn't just reflect Africa but the Caribbean as well, and the art teacher did not find it racially offensive. Again, I held my ground, repeating that this act was disrespectful to Africa and to African Americans, and that it violated the very ideals of cultural respect that the Quakers were attempting to impart through their teachings.

The principal was clearly in a quandary, but this issue with the masks was about race and I wasn't going to pretend otherwise. We hung up unresolved, with the principal saying, "Call me if you come up with anything."

I felt I already had come up with something! I'd told her: "Let's not confirm racial stereotypes and dishonor Africa by wearing African masks in a Halloween parade." I felt frustrated at not being heard, and irritated that she had thrown it back in my lap rather than coming up with a collaborative solution. But the next week the principal called to thank me and to say that the children would not be wearing the African masks. Instead, the masks would be displayed in the hallways of the school for viewing.

When I told Anique, she beamed and it lit up the world for me as I imagined the sun did long ago for children at home in Africa, before our world was clouded by the cruelty of America and slavery, before Africa lost its children and the tears of a whole nation made it rain every day. But a lingering question intruded on my vision: Why had there not been an outpouring of similar sentiments from other black families? Who do we really think is going to teach our children to have racial self-respect – the schools, or us? And who will demand racial respect for our children in social encounters? We must teach our children life-enhancing, genetic self-respect and racial pride. By example, we must challenge ourselves, schools, and other social environments to show racial respect for our children. Undefended, children can mistake their parents' silence and passivity as proof of their black inferiority. This is the worst lesson we could possibly give them.

Protecting Our Children from Racism in the Media

While watching Nickelodeon's *All That,* a kids' show, with Anique, I was appalled at the way black people were depicted. The two black males on the show were overdressed in drag, speaking Ebonics and badmouthing each other. (I accept Ebonics as one element of black life, but television would have us think it's the only way we speak). When another young black male entered the skit, the two women friends (drag queens) tried to out-do each other using violence, put-downs and lies. And when his girlfriend entered the free-for-all, she played the Angry Black Woman, using hips, hands and Ebonics to put him in his place.

Our children are listening to the voices of white supremacy through television and we are standing around with our hands tied. My niece thought I was overreacting. "But Aunt Faye," she challenged me, "what about all the blacks who wouldn't have the opportunity to be on television? Everyone on that show is silly, not just blacks."

While there are blacks who may fit these negative racial constructions, we must not confuse who they are with who they could have been. And we can argue that *The Simpsons* pokes fun at an ignorant white family on television, but white children can afford to laugh at themselves because they are born to parents in the ruling class. White children will not be uprooted from their superior position in society by absorbing a few negative ideas about whites from watching the cartoon. But it's different for black children. Already sponges for all the messages of racism hurled at them every day by our racist society, they turn on the TV and see black comedy shows like *The PJs* – which is thankfully off the air now -- that reinforce every conceivable negative stereotype ever spoken about black people. If the black shadow was a screenwriter, this is the show it would have created.

Set in the projects, black people destroy their property and steal from one another while badmouthing and criticizing one another. The cornerstones of their lives are drugs, alcohol, prostitution and unemployment. Big protruding butts, rolled lips, and voodoo add extra "nigger" flavoring. The laughter of children watching *The PJs* and shows like it is a deadly sound. Dying with each laugh is self-love, self-pride, self-image, self-confidence, self-esteem, group respect, group harmony and positive black identity. As any shred of positive sense of being black recedes, the black shadow moves from the hallways and corners of their psyches and gets a foot in the door.

Like the black actors and actresses who sacrificed their dignity for the privilege of showing their amazing talent and skills on the screen as mammies, maids and happy-go-lucky men-boys, many entertainers today are squeezed into roles that promote black self-hate. But those earlier black pioneers were supposed to be breaking barriers that would pave the way for other African Americans to follow as fully vested humans endowed with a wide range of emotions and behaviors. But like the 40 acres and a mule, America failed to keep her promise –again. So black parents, politicians, athletes, entertainers, educators and religious advisors must become stakeholders in the identity development of black children, advocating for better black TV. But what parents can do right now to protect their children from being infected with the black shadow is turn off those programs that insult black people and teach their children self-hate.

Sticks and Stones…and Names that Harm

Language is the Federal Express of delivering the lie of black inferiority. Black parents must become psychologically aware so they can hear the black shadow when it erupts in the way we talk to our children. We must also become adept in uncovering messages of black inferiority in childhood games and songs. While the old school yard song of my day – *Ennie, Meenie, Mighty Mo, Catch a nigger by his toe, If he hollers, let him go, Ennie, Meenie, Mighty Mo* – is passé, another was waiting to take its place when Anique, who is now 23, was a child.

ET, ET
ET from out of space
He had an ugly face
Sitting in a rocket
Eating Betty Crocket
Watching the clock go tic toc, tic toc
Sha-wa-da, wa-da
Tic toc
Sha-wa-da, wa-da
ABCDEFG
You better get your dirty black hands off of me
I got the moon shock, moon shock

Black-eyed peas—
Freeze!

Leaving work early one afternoon for the delight of seeing Anique, I came upon her singing the ET song in a hand game with herself. After listening in horrified silence, I gathered my thoughts and emotions. I did not want to berate or belittle Anique because of the black shadow that was walking up and down in my mind. Unwanted feelings of fear and desperation can make parents and other concerned relatives turn angry toward children, pouring salt into an already open wound.

I sat down with her and asked her to tell me about the song. Where had she learned it? What did she think it was saying about being black? Was it only black children who sang this song, or did white children also sing the ET song? Where were the teachers when the children were singing this song on the playground? Did any of the teachers say anything about the song?

Anique had learned the song from one of the other black girls in her class. She didn't know what it was saying about being black. Black and white children sang this song in their hand game. The teachers were out on the playground, but they were not listening to their songs.

I asked Anique if she thought it was fair to say "dirty black hands," but not "dirty white hands," since both black and white children participated in the game. This she thought about carefully, because at age 7, she understood the concept of fairness. She agreed that it didn't seem very fair. She was a child who believed in the tooth fairy. How could I talk to her about the appalling racism in this song?

I said gently, "You know, Anique, some people think black people are ugly and dirty just because we're black."

She nodded. Even at 7, this wasn't a new concept for her.

I continued: "I think the song would be better if we changed it around and then you could teach the new way to your friends at school."

She perked up when she realized I was going to play with her. I sang:

ET, ET
ET from out of space

He had a different face
Sitting in a rocket
Eating Betty Crocket
Watching the clock go tic toc, tic-toc
Sha-wa-da, wa-da
Tic Toc
Sha-wa-da, wa-da
ABCDEFG
You better look out before you get the moon shock
I got the moon shock, moon shock
Everybody—
Freeze!

I am astonished and distressed again and again by the songs and sayings of black children that are ballads of self-hatred. They are manifestations of the black shadow speaking through the mouths of babes, who have learned to call themselves, "nigger."

Race Lessons

"We raise our daughters and love our sons."

"God bless the child who's got her own."

"Black men ain't no good. Black women are controlling."

These are just some of the lessons taught at home and in the community that perpetuate the black shadow. With the layering of self-hate on top of racism, black children grow up learning that black equals inferior. My client Barbara Ann was successful professionally and married to a man who gave her anything she wanted, yet she still never felt good enough. Being black made her feel inferior. Feeling like an impostor at work and unworthy of her husband's love at home, Barbara Ann was depressed and anxious. For years she had tried to escape her low self-esteem by buying expensive clothes and jewelry. But the bad feelings always returned, making her feel worse each time. In therapy she found the safety, security and comfort of having someone she could confess to about her life-long feelings of shame she internalized as a dark-skinned child growing up in her southern black family. After months of excavating the memories and emotions from growing up black she was able to distinguish between her authentic self and her internalized feelings of being inferior because she was born black. She became a critical thinker and learned to stand back and look at how she'd been taught to believe blacks are inferior. She shined a light on her black shadow and consequently it had less and less power over her. When she left therapy, she was able to love herself, and from that place of self-love and self-esteem she could finally be happy in her life.

Guarding the Shadow

Children are vulnerable to losing their shaky hold on black self-worth and competence when the family is separated by degrees of blackness. It sends them confusing messages about what to love and value and respect about themselves and others. I remember working with 20-year-old Sonja, whose parents kept her away from the poor black neighborhood where they grew up. They had made it into the middle class and wanted their child to be with the "right" black element and of course with whites. Because her parents were focused on "protecting" her from lower-class blacks, they failed to see that by their choices they were communicating to Sonja that blackness was a danger and a problem. At school, Sonja was rejected by the few black males. They ignored her and dated only white girls. Feeling that there was something intrinsically wrong with her, Sonja tried to manage her low self-image through binging, purging and dieting. By college she was also using drugs to numb herself to feelings of unworthiness and self-hate.

Harvard-trained lawyer Lawrence Mungin describes in his autobiography, *The Good Black: A True Story of Race in America,* how he learned not to acknowledge racism from his parents. It was the same for Sonja. Her parents didn't want to talk about race, or their own racism, and so she was left confused and miserable. One psychiatric hospitalization later for attempted suicide, Sonja and her parents sought family therapy. As their only child, Sonja embodied all her parents' hopes for achieving racial parity and social equality through academic excellence and hard work. The parents had never talked about their own experiences with racism, instead channeling their feelings into working harder and putting more pressure on Sonja to prove that racism didn't matter as long as one achieved.

Sonja's boiling anger at having been duped into believing that all she had to do was work hard and do the right thing to be fully accepted in white America was directed at herself as a way to get back at her parents. When I finally got the family to talk about what was simmering under the surface, Sonja angrily accused them of being snobs for turning their backs on family and negatively judging other blacks.

The family is a very powerful force that holds the key to defending black children against learned black inferiority. Like the scattering four winds, learned black inferiority can come from all directions. If we open our eyes and look closely instead of looking away, we will see that racism and the lie of black inferiority is everywhere – home, community, school, church and the larger society. Black parents must be devoutly committed to learning new ways of thinking and behaving for the sake of their children's positive self-image and happy futures. I'm not underestimating the amount of energy and sheer stamina it takes to change how we think and to get rid of the pernicious myth of black inferiority in ourselves. But the more we understand how the black shadow develops in our children, the better we can interrupt and thwart it, and teach our children to do battle with it as well.

We've been divided and separated by racism, but we can heal this wound. We can stop acting like crabs in a barrel, hurting and destroying ourselves and one another. We can take back control of our own minds and teach our children how to do the same. Consider it a daily practice to expose the myth of black inferiority as a lie. Be an ally to your children and to your own soul. The black shadow is a disturbance in our minds and bodies that is in need of soul healing. Understanding the black shadow is nourishment for the soul. Break the silence and let your soul be free.

Family Exercises

The most important thing parents can do is to encourage open dialogue with their children about race, racism, the black shadow and the myth of black inferiority. Here are some ways to start the conversation.

Convene a Family Discussion Session: Gather your family together and start a conversation about the myth of black inferiority. Explain it to young children in ways they can understand and ask others for their ideas. Remember not to analyze, criticize, judge or accuse – just listen.

Start A Family Movie Club: Select movies that are age-appropriate and have each person write down three things they see in the movie that reinforce the myth of black inferiority.

Talk about our History of Slavery: Read age-appropriate books with your children about slavery and discuss how it makes everyone feel to think about those things happening to our black ancestors. Read about Harriet Tubman and Frederick Douglas and other former slaves and discuss how they overcame the myth of black inferiority.

Convene an Adult Family Meeting: Invite all the adults in the family to read Facing the Black Shadow and then identify behaviors in your family that spring from learned black inferiority. It might be how adults talk about children in the family, or the use of the N-word. Listen with an open heart and mind, without criticizing or judging. Sit a bowl on the table. Ask each person to write down a family behavior(s) related to learned black inferiority. Put it in the bowl. Take turns taking a behavior out of the bowl. The person choosing the behavior should first say what s/he thinks should be done about it. Keep going around until everyone has responded. By consensus decide on a plan of action. Review the family's progress weekly or monthly and celebrate successes!

Chapter 4
Black Women Through the Lens of Slavery

Lena Horne, Dorothy Dandridge, Beverly Johnson, Vanessa Williams, Iman, Halle Berry, Tyra Banks, Beyonce – each of these media symbols of black beauty radiates confidence and strength on the stage, the silver screen, the magazine cover. And not one of them is darker than a brown paper bag.

It's clear that the myth of black inferiority makes it hard for society to appreciate dark-skinned women as beautiful. But where exactly is the dividing line between "light-skinned" and "dark-skinned"? Most white people wouldn't even realize my sister and I are different shades of dark, but we are well aware of it. Because of racism, black people are tuned in to the subtlest differences in skin tone. My grandmother, who always felt she was ugly because she was darker than her sister, was actually Tyra Banks's complexion. Our judgments and reactions to skin tone are subjective, but nevertheless there is always a skin tone hierarchy in the room when black people are gathered. If I'm lighter than you, I automatically have more power than you in this racist world. I automatically am considered worthier, even if it's just a shade worthier. When we compare ourselves to one another, one of us always comes up dark, which is the same as saying one of us always comes out on the bottom.

After I saw a painting called "White Chocolate" at an art show, which depicted a light-skinned house slave serving the master, the therapist in me began to think more deeply about the source of this skin-color competition among black people, and especially black women. When did it start? Where does it come from? The answer was in the painting, staring me in the face: it was the rape of black women by white men that began the color divide among blacks in America.

The Double Bind of Slave Rape

Understanding and challenging skin color prejudices in black America require us to look backward while moving forward, like the Sankofa bird – a West African symbol – which flies forward while looking backward. In slavery, black women routinely were raped by their white masters. The children that resulted from these violations were often lighter-skinned than their black mothers. This was the beginning of "meaningful" skin color variations in the African American community. Because of the lie of black inferiority and the imposition of the "nigger" stereotype on blacks, many women believed it was better to have lighter-skinned babies because white was intrinsically superior to black. There was something perhaps seductive about this idea for the rape victims, who clung to the hope that their fairer offspring would have an easier life under slavery's cruel rules. But it was a confusing mindset to maintain, because it meant the sexual assault they had endured was practically an honor being bestowed on them by the white rapists.

From the master's vicious sexual abuse of black slave women came light-skinned children, and these children had greater value than dark-skinned black children. I mean that literally: a slave owner could sell a lighter slave for more money than he could a darker slave. Lightness was a valuable commodity, as were Caucasian features. After fathering light-skinned black females, white masters might reward light-skinned women with milder treatment, but of course not their freedom. Dark female slaves were taught that they were undeserving of the milder treatment given to light-skinned slave women. Light-skinned black women, on the other hand, were taught that they were only deserving of milder treatment in relation to dark-skinned black women. This set up a competition and resentment among black women. We were divided by skin tone from the days of slavery.

Darker black women still feel resentment when our lighter-skinned sisters are more successful in the mainstream. It's easier for light-skinned black actresses to get leading roles in movies for cross-over audiences. The black models who make it onto the covers of fashion and women's magazines and into advertisements for high-end products are light skinned women with distinctly European features. When the light-skinned black singer Beyonce was pictured on her album cover as a white woman (thanks to face and body make-up) and wearing a blonde wig, I felt a surge of disappointment. Being beautiful and talented isn't enough. The singer and the company executives, looking to increase profit margins, decided to pass Beyonce off as a white woman so that whites would identify with her and buy her album. It wouldn't be so serious if we weren't all living under the black shadow, where the myth of black inferiority pollutes our lives. Beyonce is a black woman, and when she passes herself off as white, it poisons the well for black women and girls who will never pass as white and who don't have Beyonce's Caucasian facial features. Appearing as a blonde-haired, white-skinned beauty, what message is role model Beyonce sending to young black women? That whiteness is still a valuable commodity, and blackness is still a liability.

But that's not the only thing that troubles me about the cover. Beyonce is posed in a black crochet monokini, a seductive Jezebel splayed out on a leopard-print couch. Is this the pose of a strong woman who owns her own sexuality, or a descendant of slaves trying hard to be an object of desire for her white masters? I wonder what her daughter, Blue Ivy Carter, will learn from this when she's old enough to feel society's gaze on her black self.

Lighter is Prettier

Children are the canaries in the coal mine when it comes to sniffing out racist assumptions. There was a famous doll test conducted with black children in the late 1930s and early 1940s by black psychologists Kenneth and Mamie Clark. They found that children as young as 3 years old preferred white dolls over black dolls. In the late 1980s, black psychologists Darlene Powell Hopson and Derek S. Hopson found that black children still felt white dolls were "prettier," "cleaner" and "nicer." This tells me it's an uphill battle for black women to look in the mirror and see our black faces and think, "Pretty!"

The encouraging news is that the Hopsons discovered that black children could unlearn the myth of black inferiority through open discussions about racism along with positive modeling and reinforcement of the positive attributes of blackness. After the children engaged in these discussions, the percentage who chose black dolls nearly doubled, and the number who thought the black doll was ugly decreased by more than a third. While this is hopeful news, more recent studies of the doll test with children of all races show an overwhelming preference among children for the white or lighter-skinned doll.

This aspect of the black shadow is very difficult to talk about because our feelings about beauty are masked behind denial, secrecy, shame, embarrassment and even defensiveness. In *The Color Complex: The Politics of Skin Color Among African Americans,* Kathy Russell, Midge Wilson and Ronald Hall write: "Throughout American history degrees of skin coloring and kinkiness of hair have had the power to shape the quality of black people's lives. Social scientists have advanced various theories to explain the widespread preference for light skin and straighter features. The first theory contends that the 'establishment' sets standards for behavior and appearance and that those who strive for success must conform accordingly. Standards change only after enough members of a subordinate group have moved into positions of power."

Degree of lightness, more than any other factor, is still the measure of a black woman's beauty, according to her own judgment and society's. "Tyra Banks is an example of black beauty to me," said a young woman named Antoinette during a workshop I taught on racism. "And I think the reason why is because the first people who I thought were pretty were white. And they had long hair. So the black women with the lightest skin and the straightest, longest hair looked the prettiest to me." I noticed that Antoinette's own hair was short, and her skin was dark brown. How could she ever feel beautiful if Tyra Banks was her ideal?

The fact that black women believe that lighter is prettier is both embarrassing and controversial for us. A very distraught black mother came up to me after I gave a presentation on black female identity issues at a conference in the nation's capitol. She was at her wit's end because her young daughter had been begging and whining and pleading for a white doll. The mother had tried reasoning with the child about the virtues of her own physical beauty, but the child was relentless: she had to have a white doll. The mother was experiencing battle fatigue and was on the verge of giving in to the daughter's inexplicable longing. To the mother, her daughter's obsession with owning a white doll was baffling. She had tried to instill positive racial identity in her daughter by telling her that she was beautiful every day since the day she was born. I wondered silently if this mother, who herself was dark-skinned, had dealt with her own issues around beauty and acceptance. Or had she mouthed the words, "You're beautiful," each day to a daughter who sensed the mother's lack of self-respect? What real chance is there for a little black girl to develop positive black female identity – even with a collection of black dolls – if her mother and "other mothers" (caregivers, aunts, extended family) give her contradictory messages?

Beautiful Baby

"Tiara had a wide nose and brown skin like her father when she was born," Vivian said in a cracking voice. She stared at her hands, remembering. "I used to like his brown skin, but suddenly I didn't like brown anymore when I looked at my daughter's tiny brown face. And when my mother said nothing more than she was 'ashy and wrinkled,' I hated brown even more. I felt so guilty about hating brown that I let my daughter get away with many things. I was easy on her because I was afraid of being too hard on her because of her skin color. I still feel guilty, and Tiara is a grown woman with a 5-year-old son of her own."

Thanks to the myth of black inferiority, skin color is the central defining measure of a black woman's beauty, intelligence, goodness and self-worth. Before we can see the world around us, we're bombarded with the consequences of our skin color. Will a grandmother's eyes light up when she first sees her dark-skinned grandbaby? Will she coo, "You pretty baby!" Will we be told we're good, clean, lovely and desirable? Or will we be dismissed as ugly, bad, dirty, untrustworthy and inferior because of our dark skin? These instinctive judgments don't have to be spoken; they pass to us as silently as a handshake. For black girls, we understand that we have been assigned to a plus or minus column on the beauty scale because of our skin.

Black women and girls have little respite from the black shadow that never lets us forget our place in a white-dominated world, a world where we are programmed to feel second best – "niggers." The myth of black inferiority tells us that light skin is beauty; dark skin is misfortune. Is it any wonder why a little black girl would long for a white doll? When children play, they pretend they are someone they're not. She can pretend she's white and imagine what it's like to feel pretty and admired.

Good Hair

"Do y'all remember Whoopi Goldberg when she did stand-up comedy?" asked 49 year-old Sheilah during a discussion I facilitated on racism and black women's identity. "She took something and wrapped it around her head so it would look like long hair. I remember doing that long before Whoopi came around. So one of the things I associated with beauty was absolutely long hair."

"Yeah," said 24-year-old Kimberly. "I remember standing in front of the mirror with the towel hanging down my back because I wanted my hair long and I wanted it straight."

"I remember sitting in my mother's kitchen and her pressing my hair and saying, 'You're going to be so beautiful when I finish getting all the naps out'," 25-year-old Simone chimed in. "And I would say, 'I can't wait for my hair to be pressed out because it's going to be so long.' I would just imagine how straight it was going to be. And to me it was like I had to go through these stepping stones to get to this image of myself as a beautiful little girl because of this straight hair."

"When I was in the first grade, I had this friend Desiree who was light with long hair," another participant, Lindsay, reminisced. "And I remember we both liked this little boy, but he told me he did not want to play with me because my hair wasn't long like hers. So I got upset. I went home crying and mother said, 'Well you know these things are going to happen and it doesn't mean you're not pretty. You have to be pretty to yourself.' She gave me the best lecture she could, I guess, trying to make me feel better. But I went upstairs and cut the hair off every Barbie and any other doll that had long hair. My mother was shocked when she came in my room. 'What did you do?' And I said, 'If I don't have long hair, I don't want my dolls to have long hair.' From then on, I wouldn't play with dolls with long hair, all because of that one incident with that little boy. I have carried that pain to this day." Lindsay stopped being friends with Desiree, too, because Desiree had become one of "them" with long hair.

Unable to remove black skin from our backs, black women focus heavily on altering nature's other folly: knotty, nappy, kinky, peasy, beady, bad hair. Wanting female beauty because it opens the door to visibility, acknowledgment, security and acceptance, large numbers of us have fried, dyed, weaved and hidden our natural hair behind wigs in our attempt to move up on the beauty totem pole. The blonde revolution happening in black America is our latest attempt to feel more beautiful and be judged more worthy. Even those of us wearing natural hairstyles, but dyed blonde, are still chasing beauty.

Comedian Chris Rock produced an extraordinary documentary called Good Hair, which offered black America an opportunity to witness black women's struggle with slavery's image of us as ugly in our black skin and kinky hair. His film showed black women from all walks of life and every shade of color in pursuit of good hair. Light skin and good hair were once thought to be synonymous in the black community, but in this documentary we saw light-skinned black women purchasing good hair alongside dark-skinned black women.

A private screening of Good Hair was sponsored in Philadelphia. I was invited to share in a panel discussion afterward. It should come as no surprise that the conversation quickly turned away from the real issue of internalized black inferiority. Instead, black women defensively justified their obsession with changing their natural hair.

"I'm an actress and have to do what Hollywood requires."

"I'm in television news and must look presentable and relatable."

"I'm looking for a job, so I have to look the part for white employers."

All of these justifications focused on the external, and I wanted us to talk about the internal – what goes on inside us that makes us reject our own bodies? No one but me wanted to talk about our internalized black inferiority. I was given hostile looks when I suggested that our obsession with changing our hair is a problem we inherited from slavery. What I was saying was too dangerous for people to hear in that moment. I was asking them to face the black shadow that makes us uncomfortable in our own skin and hair.

The ugly truth is that most black people seldom realize that the myth of black inferiority is such an active, constant force in their lives. It's easier to see the problems of racism that come from white institutions and white people in positions of power and authority. Looking at our internalized racism can be terrifying at first. But we won't be free until we do it. Hair is just one example of how we twist ourselves up inside and out, spend money we can't and shouldn't have to afford on products and services to try to make our hair less "nigger" and more white. Watching the *Black Girls Rock Awards* show on BET (Black Entertainment Television), I wanted to cry. Black Girls Rock was established to promote positive self-image and self-worth for black girls. Yet nearly every visible black woman had crowned her head with "good" hair – the kind that comes from India and Asia – as we learned in the movie *Good Hair*. It was definitely not the black kind. How can we expect black girls to gain positive self-esteem and value themselves when what we show them are black women rejecting their own bodies and trying to look like white women?

The myth of black inferiority makes us automatically believe long, straight hair (white women's hair) is superior to our natural nappy black hair. Like the patch of poison ivy that takes over more of the garden year after year if it's not uprooted, the unchallenged idealization of whites and their cultural imperatives spreads and causes us more problems. With each new generation of blacks, the cumulative effects of negative learning from internal conflicts over skin color and hair intensify, solidifying our unconscious acceptance of white superiority and black inferiority.

I do believe some things have changed for the better for black women. We rarely say anymore, "She's beautiful, for a dark-skinned girl." But a belief in our own beauty doesn't reach our souls. Chris Rock's movie showed us that we still don't feel beautiful enough in our own black bodies and that we don't appreciate our diverse black beauty because the racist world doesn't. It's time to look at and question our own behavior.

I was a semi-finalist in 2003, for the Robert Wood Johnson Health Policy Fellowship that would take me to Congress. I really wanted this fellowship, and I was nervous about being rejected so I allowed self-doubt (my own and others) about my natural hair to make me go against my gut. I straightened it for my interview before a panel of judges in Washington, D.C. I had been selected as a semi-finalist based on my written proposal, but in the interview I would be judged in person. My black shadow told me that I might be mistaken for a "nigger" with my natural hair. They would see it and immediately decide I was not good enough.

The problem was that with my straightened hair, I did not feel my genuine self, and during the interview I was not relaxed and engaged. I was not selected.

The next year, I reapplied and was again selected as a semi-finalist. By that time, I was in the process of locking my hair, so this time I went to the interview in locks. I went to the second interview feeling like I was presenting my authentic self and it made me feel comfortable in my own body. My interview reflected my self-confidence and I was selected. I was proud to be the first couple and family therapist to receive the prestigious fellowship, and to know I had received it not because I tried to look more like a white person, but because I was myself.

There was another twist to this hair story. My boyfriend, Richard, had been telling me that I needed to perm "that mess" prior to my interview. He didn't like my locks, and on some days he referred to my natural hair as "nigger knots." When he said that, I was furious and wanted to kick him out. But on another level I understood that Richard was uncomfortable with my natural hair because he felt like he was with a "nigger" woman when my shoulder-length permed hair became a two-inch natural. Like all of us, he had been indoctrinated in the myth of black inferiority, so it was a challenge for him to overcome his fear and aversion to a black woman's natural hair.

Learning to love our hair despite its long association as a "nigger" marker requires tolerance and patience. I had to resist my own fears that my hair would mark me as a "nigger" and that I wouldn't be chosen when I went to the first interview. I strengthened my resolve to remember that beauty is a state of mind and not the condition of my hair when I left that first interview, and it was this that allowed me to know and appreciate my worth when I went to the second interview. It is our state of mind that has everything to do with the superior white image and the inferior black self.

Selling Beauty

The fashion and cosmetic industry is racism and sexism personified. Women's dreams are manipulated, toyed with and broken by the cruel world of beauty. Black women are denied entrance in the marketplace where women are auctioned off the beauty block, the highest bid going for young, thin, sexy, submissive-looking white females. As a rule, the beauty credentialing agents don't endorse black women as beautiful unless they look nearly white.

The beauty industry preys on insecurity, and therefore it makes a killing on black women. Black hair-care products promise straight, softly curly, and/or long hair. It's the same hair we see staring back at us from the pages of magazines and the television and movie screens. Such images are so embedded in our psyches that we can conjure them up on hearing about the latest hair wonder oil or miracle growth product. The black media is a co-conspirator in the marketing of false pride and identity because of their dependency on advertising revenue. Consequently, we're caught in a viscous cycle of identity destruction in the African American community.

Fortunately for the hair care industry, but not so fortunate for black female identity, black women can rent beauty simply by pouring on a little color, adding some length, and/or removing the kinks with a perm. And what does this all mean? It means hair care is a booming business that benefits from our internalized belief in black inferiority. The black shadow is sitting right over us while we spend hours and dollars at the hair salon, while we walk the aisles of the drug store looking for a "solution" to our hair "problem."

Self-esteem and positive racial identity won't be found in chemical relaxers and hair coloring with names like "African Pride." We will have to face our black shadows and unlearn the negative messages about our black physical characteristics. Let's stop chasing the white man's fantasy of beauty and focus our energy on real change

– not just putting on a sweater when the thermostat is broken, but fixing the thermostat. Let us begin to talk openly and honestly with one another about our beauty issues. We don't need to pay for the straightest hair possible to feel beautiful; we need to face the lie of black inferiority that makes us feel ugly. The minute we throw away the white yardstick for beauty, we can invest our money in ourselves in a much more fruitful way: IRA, college fund, mortgage, paying off debts.

The struggle to achieve a male ideal of beauty is not just a black woman's issue, of course. Women of all races struggle with measuring up to that impossible ideal. But black women have a double jeopardy because we will never be white. We can never compete with white women. We are, by racism's definition, uglier because we are dark-skinned. So what can we do? First, we can take back the definition of "beauty" and redefine it to embrace our darkest sisters. We can forge strong alliances with other women and come up with our own definitions of beauty and more authentic ways to measure our worth. We can stop making negative comments and nurturing secret resentments about one another because of appearance, choosing instead genuine connection. With individual and collective will, we can look on the black shadow and expose its racism and sexism. To be free, we need to have conviction, and we need to have soul. Only by unmasking the black shadow will we be free to explore and accept our inner selves. To realize our beauty, inside and out, we must see that it is our own shadow standing in the way. To redeem ourselves, we must expose the lie of black inferiority.

The Beauty Measuring Stick

You may be thinking, "It's not that bad, Marlene. You exaggerate." I agree that there has been incremental change in the attitude toward black beauty since the black power movement of the 1970s. And yes, a few dark-skinned black models appear on mainstream magazine covers from time to time. A handful of dark-skinned black women sit in the anchor's chair of some newsrooms. Black dolls are abundantly available, though many look like the white Barbie painted brown. The once-common phrase, "She's pretty, for a dark-skinned girl," is rarely said publicly. But even so, light-skinned black women and girls are described much more often as "beautiful" than their dark sisters.

Since the beginning of slavery, when light-skinned female slaves were given a higher position in the master's home as house slaves, dark and light-skinned

African American women have engaged in a reciprocal shadow projection process. That means light-skinned and dark-skinned black women mutually blame one another for our beauty woes. Dark black women accuse light black women of thinking they are better, and light black women accuse dark black women of being jealous and wanting what they have. Hence we project our feelings about beauty onto one another when we should recognize that we are all victims of the lie of black inferiority.

Each of us defends against and rationalizes our pain. Internalizing the value system of the "master and mistress," black women were brainwashed to hold an ideal image of the pale-skinned, blue-eyed white woman as the epitome of feminine beauty. And since the female slave could never be white, the next highest aspiration for a slave was to be "light, bright, and damn-near white." Thus, light-skinned black women became desirable runners-up in the race to beauty. But no black woman, no matter how light, is going to win that race because black is still inferior to white in the dominant imagination.

Light-skinned sisters know that their reign is short-lived, lasting only until white women, who are the real queens, show up to repossess the crown. Thus, light-skinned black women were never really exempted from the less-worthy status. The ever-present "tar brush" could be engaged at white society's convenience. No matter how many octoroon and quadroon balls were held, a mulatress was always sentenced to life as a tragic mulatto. The Thomas Jefferson-Sally Hemings controversy raised this issue dramatically for contemporary white people, who questioned Hemings's character (she was "mistress" to a married man!) instead of understanding that she was a slave at the mercy of a master who chose to rape her and father children on her, and who didn't acknowledge those children as his own. It was harder for white people to grasp the truth that Hemings – the half-sister of Jefferson's white wife – was never more than a black woman to Jefferson, no matter how often she bore his children. She was not his mistress, because that would imply she was free to choose. She was property he had inherited when he married his wife.

The Three Masks of Black Womanhood

Female beauty is a convoluted issue in American society. In a male-dominated (sexist) society, beauty is linked to protection and security. Since black women are excluded from the beauty contest, we are less likely to have protection or security from either white or black America. Female beauty is also equated with submissiveness, which is the preferred position for women in a male-dominant society. In our racist society, black women are given three choices of roles to take, each of which comes right from slavery and post-slavery racism. We can be "the strong black woman," (Mammy); "the angry black woman," (Sapphire); or "the slutty black woman" (Jezebel). Black women in general and dark-skinned black women in particular are associated with one of these unflattering categories.

Wearing the strong black woman mask, a black woman doesn't need the protection and security of beauty. She can go it alone. The strong black woman never tires, can always lend a helping hand, doesn't need help raising her children and doesn't trust a man to show up for her. But behind the mask is the vulnerable black woman who feels invisible to all but God, disappearing even from herself.

Janet experienced a crack in her strong black woman (Mammy) mask when she caught her fiancé cheating. Feeling depressed, Janet came to see me on the recommendation of a friend. Janet kept telling me she didn't depend on other people; other people depended on her. She said she wasn't used to having negative feelings because she had a positive outlook on life. Also, she had faith in God. Looking at the box of tissues on the table in my office, Janet said flatly, "Don't expect me to cry." I told her that it was not my expectation but that I would understand if she did cry.

After a few sessions, Janet opened up about more than her cheating fiancé. She felt financially used by her family, who then talked badly about her behind her back. She felt demeaned on her job as a black woman in her white-male-dominated engineering job. Janet had not felt particularly loved by her fiancé, but she was nearing 40 and thought she should marry. As a dark-skinned black woman, she didn't feel like she had many options.

I talked to Janet about the black shadow and the Mammy mask. Janet immediately saw herself in the description, and it motivated her to make changes with her family. She began by setting boundaries with her brother and sister. She was willing to make a loan with a repayment plan in an emergency, but she was no longer willing to give money just because they wanted (not needed) something. She also began making plans for a career change since she was not happy as an engineer.

CHAPTER 4 – BLACK WOMEN THROUGH THE LENS OF SLAVERY

Since slavery, it has been commonplace for black women to be treated as the Mammy by black men and women and by the white world. Mammies are good for following orders and yielding to the wishes of others without any expectation of tender, loving care. This is the price she has to pay for not being beautiful – for not being white. A Mammy can wear the mask proudly but be unaware of the price she's paying in mental and physical health. Inside, an unheard whisper asks, "Ain't I a woman too?"

One major obstacle to retiring the strong black woman mask is black women's perpetual feeling of not being wanted. For black women to closely examine the strong black woman phenomenon that results in self-alienation and estrangement from others, we would have to undergo the terrifying experience of revealing our fear of being the one who is not chosen. Rejected and cast out as maids, servants and caretakers of others, black women experience the shame and stigma of being seen as unlovable – good only for cleaning up the mess left behind by others. Between give and take, she's been conditioned to give, believing others more worthy than herself. Plagued by the inner voice echoing through time to remind her of the "nigger wench" branding of slavery, she covers herself in the strong black woman mask, colluding with both racism and the black shadow.

Repeating history, in an unconscious state of being, we slip into slavery's sexualized and objectified image of us as Jezebels – what I call the slut mask. With her "big butt and thighs" to top off her black skin, the African American woman has not had a place of positive distinction on the American beauty scene. Seen as ugly and therefore a thing of ill repute, she has been over-sexualized and used for the non-committal pleasure of first white and then black men. Isolated by her unique beauty from the rest of American women, it has been easier for both white and black men to objectify, rape, batter and abuse her. The projected slutty image of her from the book of slavery justifies her mistreatment and devaluation.

Jezebels typically believe that they have to "work what you got." Dropping it like it's hot in videos and on the big screen, they mistake objectification for desirability and admiration. Confident in the slut mask, a Jezebel feels wanted, and this dynamic reaches all the way back to slavery, where black women were valued for sex and breeding. To her, sex is power; her fifteen minutes in the spotlight doesn't make it down the aisle. (This is not meant to be a joke. Look at black marriage statistics.)

Slavery's image of the black woman as a Jezebel is still big business. The plantation has been replaced by the entertainment industry, where black women are represented as prostitutes. The Jezebel mask is the black female entertainer's permit to work. Also, in a market with dwindling resources – eligible black men – it's something to be chosen, even if it's not to be the wife.

Dinah was a beautiful young woman in my opinion, but she didn't see herself that way. She had very poor self-esteem and believed her only value was between her legs. When we talked about her sense of herself, she told me she wasn't beautiful because she was "too dark." She came to see me because she was sleeping with a succession of married and single white and black men and was surprised each time that the relationship didn't work out. What she wanted more than anything was to feel loved, but she didn't know any other way to go about finding affection other than having sex. She was able to pretend to herself that they cared about her while they were in bed, but when it became clear that they were just using her for sex she grew depressed.

Dinah was intelligent, but she was also naive. She didn't see how the black shadow had unconsciously led her to adopt the Jezebel mask. From her promiscuous behavior, she might be judged a "slut," but Dinah was a young woman filled with typical dreams of love, marriage, motherhood and a house with a white picket fence. Her strategy for trying to meet her needs was failing miserably, and we worked together to help her understand how the black shadow was misleading her. Dinah realized that she was not going to find her dream by playing the Jezebel, and then she had to grapple with her wounded self-esteem as a dark-skinned woman and see how her belief that she wasn't beautiful made her feel that she would never be worthy of love. Eventually, Dinah learned to see herself as beautiful and worthy of love and her promiscuous behavior stopped.

Every smart black woman that I know is forced at some point in her life into the mask of the angry black woman, Sapphire. Women who have both beauty and brains are threatening in a sexist society, and if that woman also happens to be black, she is by definition a challenge to the white, male power structure. Smart black women are trussed into the straight jacket of Sapphire in and out of our homes. Accused of being angry and controlling, the smart black woman is exiled to a lonely place within herself, without the benefit of male protection or moral support. Others are encouraged to abandon, avoid and silence her. Not being submissive, she bears the defective stamp of womanhood.

Annette, a physician, came to therapy with her husband, Bill, a lawyer who had taken the bar exam three times and failed each one. Bill accused Annette of being unsupportive and controlling. Annette fired back that Bill refused to help with the kids even though he wasn't working. Bill was from the black middle class and Annette was from a working-class black family. Bill expected Annette to be more submissive like his stay-at-home mother. When Annette failed to go along with Bill's unilateral decisions on family matters – like sending their son to private school even though they couldn't afford it – Bill forced Annette into the Sapphire mask. Secretly, Bill saw Annette as being one of those angry, lower-class, black women despite being a physician. His suspicion was supported by the fact that Annette was beginning to sound like an angry black woman! She was unhappy and had gained a lot of weight in the last year. Recognizing that she was depressed, she decided to postpone couples therapy and seek individual therapy with another therapist.

Grappling with poor self-esteem and self-concept because we have internalized the angry black woman and a way of life that tells us we will never fit the standard for female beauty along with its rights and benefits, we hold more tightly to the angry black woman mask. We know well the message, "God bless the child who's got her own," and we don't expect anyone to have our backs. The angry black woman is often referred to as a black bitch, but no matter what people say about the word "bitch" standing for "a broad in total control of herself," she knows it's meant to be an insult.

It's so much more dangerous to be black. From a black perspective, it's dangerous because we have so little support; it's dangerous from a white perspective because of the "nigger" lie. Therefore, the black bitch and a white bitch are not equivalent. When we wear the Sapphire mask, we can't risk vulnerability. We end up eroding possibilities for close, intimate relationships because we feel abandoned and alone, and trust is too vulnerable when we're fighting to survive.

Healing

Good hair and skin color are twin planks in the myth of black inferiority. Good hair is the shield that many African American women use to pump up a flagging self-image or to inflate a weak ego. We feel less human, less beautiful, and less important with our own natural hair. Good hair is our offering to the black shadow, but we pay for that offering in human dignity, self-respect and self-acceptance.

It is the indelible mark of "nigger" that underscores our obsession with skin color and good hair. Using the good hair and/or skin color shield against black shame only takes us farther away from an authentic self. Victim to the myths of black women as Mammies, Jezebels and Sapphires – ugly, "nigger" wenches – we remain in a deep psychological vacuum, prey to the eventual fate of fatherless households, teenage pregnancy, academic failure, poverty, violence, crime, substance abuse, poor mental and physical health and incarceration.

Skin color and hair are armor for the black shadow. The black shadow is the evil mirror that tells us the "fairest of them all" is snow white, lily white, whiter than we can ever be. Self-hating black women are at risk for being exploited by predatory men, and they are in danger of turning the hate on themselves in physically destructive ways. Self-hating and ashamed, we lose our chance to have genuine connection and community with other black women, which would bring us happiness and a sense of personal power. Divided by skin color and hair, black women are recruited into self-loathing and sister-back-stabbing behaviors.

Far too often, black women find themselves feeling hopeless, helpless and unfulfilled in life. Many have slow-burning rage that weakens the soul and strains the spirit by mid-life. Black women, as a group, have been overlooked as beautiful, not living up to the dominant culture's particular kind of beauty. And many have had their dreams of being valued as women go up in smoke because they haven't felt good enough to demand better treatment from black men, from their families and the white world.

I don't believe all black women are screwed up because of what slavery did to us. The purpose of bringing slavery's images of black women into modern-day focus is not to suggest that all black women fit into either the Mammy, Jezebel or Sapphire masks. The point is to increase our awareness of slavery's limited roles for black women, and to see how those limitations still impact us today. When we become aware that we've been assigned one of these roles as a legacy of slavery and continuing racism, we can choose not to accept it.

Oprah Winfrey is a model of defiance of society's negative stereotypes of black women. Oprah has shared with the world her struggles with the effects of sexual abuse, obesity and teenage pregnancy. But Oprah didn't internalize these experiences as her failures for being a black woman. All of us have times in our lives when we have refused to remain trapped by the lie of black inferiority and claimed our right to be our authentic selves. No one is perfect, not even Oprah, but I admire her as someone determined consciously to work at realizing her full potential in body, mind and spirit. She is dedicated to living her best life – not what you or I think she should do – but guided by her own indomitable spirit. And then she reaches back and helps us do the same.

As black women, we have to refuse to be trapped in the Mammy, Jezebel and Sapphire masks, but we can also claim the positive aspects of each. From the Mammy mask, we have caring. From the Jezebel mask, we have sexuality. And from the Sapphire mask, we have assertiveness. Together, these qualities can help to bring us wholeness. A caring black woman who's accepting and responsible for her sexuality and willing to assert her needs is my definition of a healthy black woman. She is a loving partner, friend, daughter, sister and mom, and she loves herself and makes choices that are self-nurturing as well. Every black woman has the capacity for this kind of health.

Humans need possibilities, not cages. In slavery, our identity as black women was caged by whites. When you face your black shadow and claim your rightful womanhood, you will be free to discover the variety and range of your authentic self. It's time for black women to make a conscious choice to reject the black shadow's masks of Mammy, Jezebel and Sapphire. We're not caricatures or stereotypes: we're diverse, beautiful, gifted, kind and intelligent human beings who deserve dignity and respect no matter what we look like. We can't raise sons who respect women, or daughters who respect themselves until we respect ourselves enough to stop letting the myth of black inferiority chain us to wrong notions of beauty and worth. When rapper Jay-Z and Beyonce's daughter was born, Jay-Z decided not to use the word "bitch" in song anymore. We each need our own wake-up call, our own reason to bury the stereotypes that oppress us. Start with Mammy, Jezebel, and Sapphire.

Exercises for Black Women

Set aside some quiet time to do the following exercises. Write your thoughts and findings in a notebook or journal, and invite family members to participate.

Step 1: Draw a family tree that tracks your family's beliefs and patterns about skin color. Ask each family member, from oldest to youngest, to identify the spoken and unspoken skin color beliefs he or she experiences in the family. Ask about skin color beliefs from outside that affect family members, and what each person thinks the family could do to stop promoting the "less than/better than" mentality that is often present with skin color assignment.

Step 2: Develop a list of up to five adjectives to describe each family member. If you have trouble coming up with adjectives, think of family stories that people like to tell about those family members. Do any themes emerge along skin color lines? Consider what beliefs you took to heart and their impact on your self-image and self-worth.

Step 3: Get in touch with your unconscious self and the shadowy feelings you have about skin color and beauty by starting to notice your reactions, feelings and beliefs. Write them down. Here are questions to ask yourself:

- **Annoyance!** Which black women's masks tend to get on your nerves? What is it about the Mammy, Jezebel or Sapphire that makes you crazy? How do you relate to these same things in yourself? How does it make you feel to think you have "their" qualities? What would you do to fix it?

- **Admiration!** Who are the black women you admire? What do you like about them? Do you have their same qualities? What would you use these qualities to do in your life if you had them? Could you be overlooking these things in yourself?

- **Assumptions!** Do you identify as light, brown, or dark-skinned? How do others identify your skin color? List as many stereotypes as you can remember that are associated with people who are your color. How do you feel about each one? Repeat for the other two. How do these stereotypes affect you when you're around other black women? (Recalling or renting the movie School Daze could serve as a catalyst for answering this question.)

- **Allure!** Choose three black women you consider beautiful. What makes them beautiful? How did your family define black beauty? Do you feel pretty? What would make you feel pretty? Create your own standard of beauty, just for you.

- **Awareness!** What physical characteristics do you assume black men look for in black women? How close or far are you from that physical appearance? How does it make you act in relationships? Does it affect what you expect from men? How does it make you feel about the women who look this way?

- **Agreement!** Write your own, personal contract. Decide which personal behaviors you want to change when it comes to skin color. For example, you might want to stop using "light-skin" or "dark-skin" to describe another black person. Reward yourself for making progress, but don't punish yourself for backsliding. This is meant to be positive all around. Ask yourself daily, "How am I doing?"

Step 4: Have a mother/daughter, or sister/sister, or friend/friend heart-to-heart talk about all your new realizations about the black shadow and your sense of self. Encourage all the black women and girls you know to talk about race, including skin color issues in black America. Make this your mission! Use discussions of books and movies to facilitate these conversations. Embrace the emotional tension that may come up and have courage. It's hard to talk about being black, but it's easier if we help one another.

Chapter 5
Shadow-Boxing with the Boy

Chained together in human waste through the long voyage from home, family and friends, African men who were captured and sold as slaves lost more than just their freedom. They lost their fundamental male identities as fathers, husbands, brothers, sons, leaders, providers and protectors. Black men were transformed from self-respecting human beings to property with a penis that could perform the master's work and breed more slaves for the master. The roles that distinguish boys from men were denied to slaves – leader, father, husband – leaving black men developmentally stunted. The white man called him "boy" and the grown black slave bowed his head and did the master's bidding. Black manhood was forced into the shadow, and still today the black man's confusion about manhood and self-respect forms the core of his black shadow. We see the fallout in the high rates of divorce among African Americans, in high rates of absentee fathers, and the high rates of incarceration and addiction among black men.

The strong sense of connection and responsibility that black men felt to women and children in Africa was forbidden during slavery. It's important to understand that connection prevents alienation from both self and others. Estranged from self and family, black men were left with shameful feelings of inadequacy and guilt for not being able to take care of their families. Today, black men face higher drop-out rates and rates of unemployment, and if they try at all, it's a struggle to support their families. They watch themselves fail, and that sense of inadequacy, pain and suppressed rage builds up until far too many numb it through drugs, violence, workaholism, sex, anger, isolation and depression. Prison is a form of isolation for many black men, and so many of our brothers are locked up behind bars with more joining them every year.

Black men have a hard road to walk before they can feel inside themselves that they are no longer "boy," but are fully empowered as grown men. Until that happens, men are unavailable for healing. They're caught in their black shadows, which make it hard to be present for their children, achieve their goals and nurture their ambitions, commit to relationships and stay monogamous. The psychological toll on them by the black shadow is disengagement and alienation. Their souls are crying out for help.

Work and Black Male Identity

"I live in fear of professional rejection, of not being accepted," confided 34-year-old Keith. "Early on, I attended white schools where I was not thought to have equal intelligence. All my life, I've tried to overcome the perception of color by trying to be excellent. But I always worry that I haven't done my best. On the job, I'm so afraid of messing up or getting into conflict that I'm often conciliatory when I shouldn't be. I don't even know who I am. I began imitating white folks when I was in middle school. I see someone who I think is smart do a certain thing and then I adopt that behavior. I learned to talk like a white boy from one of my teachers. I don't feel comfortable in my own skin. I feel like I'm on stage all the time."

When Keith came to therapy, he was having marital problems. After dating only white women in college Keith found a "Mrs. Right" black woman. What attracted him most to her was her intelligence and ambition. But the fact that she was climbing the economic ladder while he was stuck a few rungs below became the cause of conflict in their marriage. Both Keith and his wife had expected him to be the main breadwinner, and his wife was disappointed that it wasn't so. She accused him of not having enough ambition and drive. Keith heard her criticisms as confirmation of his male inadequacy, adding to his fear of not measuring up to his white colleagues. That made him shy away from taking more professional risks, like challenging a co-worker and being more outspoken in meetings. Keith withdrew at work and home and felt depressed.

Therapy was Keith's wife's idea. She was seeing a psychologist and wanted Keith to get help, too. Keith only agreed to it after his wife asked him to move out of the house. It took him a few sessions to start to trust me, and then he opened up and described years of pain and suffering from constantly trying to out-box his boy shadow. Was he man enough? Would he ever feel what he imagined "real" men felt: self-confident, proud and strong?

Talking about the black shadow helped him to stop undermining his own self-confidence with the idea that he was naturally flawed as a black man. He looked at how he had internalized the myth of black inferiority, and also the patriarchal idea that men should not have feelings, should not be emotional and should not need love or caring, but only sex. Keith felt liberated to talk about these topics that had been sources of shame and insecurity. He began to talk more openly and honestly with male friends whom he thought were also shadow-boxing themselves into corners. It was refreshing to be able to voice some of their fears and confusion and give one another support. I helped Keith to understand that all black men are burdened with the history of humiliation and attending feelings of inferiority as a result of what happened to our ancestors when they were enslaved.

Work and Manhood

The need to be accepted, validated, and treated as a worthwhile man is at the heart of the black man's story in America. Over the years, a number of college-educated and gifted black men have floated through the doors of my office to talk about employment problems. While nearly all reported dealing with some form of discrimination and racism at their previous jobs, their strategies for responding to those injustices varied. There were those who quietly left and those who quit in anger. But no matter how they handled it, every single one of them experienced overriding feelings of inferiority as men.

Work is a shame issue in the black male community that can be traced back to the tree of slavery. There it hangs, along with the many other branches that sweep across our lives without us knowing that we're caught in the tangle of past. We tell ourselves and one another that slavery is dead and done with, yet we still carry the burden of that tragedy. In Africa, men were expected to feed, house and protect their families. It was in slavery that black men lost the means and freedom to do this. It wasn't a result of laziness, lack of work ethic or lack of ambition. Denying black men the right to provide for their beloveds was a systematic way that white slave owners broke the spirits and stole the strength of black men. No group of men or women has worked harder in America than the black slaves, whose broken backs made their masters rich, fueled the textile industries in the north (which created jobs for white immigrants) and built the

United States into a great nation. But black men received no wages or profit for their labors. They didn't even receive acknowledgement for their hard work. As America delivered on her promise for a better life for waves of white immigrants, black men stayed at the bottom of the pecking order. If they were lucky enough to have a job, they could expect the lowest pay, the longest hours, the worst working conditions and the most abuse by their employers. And they could expect to be stuck in that position no matter how hard they worked, how much ambition they had or how willing they were to learn new skills. Black men remained "boy" while their white counterparts moved up and on to better things.

The "nigger" stereotype followed black men out of slavery and into the workplace. My black male clients described the constant frustration of working hard, only to have doors slammed in their faces, and then hearing their white managers blame them for being irresponsible, lazy or just not quite good enough. These messages echo the black shadow that whispers to them, "Inferior black man."

Men in America measure their self-worth by their bank accounts, which brings them status and power. A black man who has no money and no opportunity to earn any suffers from negative self-worth. Even though he is well aware of the realities of racism and knows he's been discriminated against, he still feels inferior as a man. He internalizes his economic failure and it becomes a source of tremendous guilt, shame and envy. Some black men even blame black women for their economic failure, not understanding that racism, not black women, is the problem. For instance, 28-year-old David told me that black women's success was actually part of a larger plot to emasculate black men. "Because the desire is really to emasculate black men, to strip them of their manhood, keep them out of the decent paying positions, they let the black woman move up the corporate ladder much more quickly. So you got all these black women getting paid, and you got these black guys who ain't making what they have the capability to make. So therefore when you and me hook up, you believe you're in charge of the household. And I think this is what strips a lot of us of our self worth. You think, 'I can't even take care of my own household.' That throws off the balance of power."

My client, Keith, had been unconsciously feeling this way. In therapy one day, he came to a realization that changed his marriage dynamic. He recognized that he was not only envious that his wife was more advanced in her career than he was and made more money than he did, but he was blaming her for his feeling of male inferiority. He'd accused her of being "castrating," instead of truly understanding how his boy shadow was struggling with feelings of inferiority. Once he saw this pattern that he was playing out, he was able to stop seeing his wife as the problem and start looking at how the myth of black inferiority and his black shadow were real problems he had to deal with.

"The Player" Mask

Just as black women wear stereotypical masks of black womanhood – Sapphire, Jezebel and Mammy – so, too, do black men wear stereotypical masks of black manhood. These are not flattering depictions of black men, and just as I didn't suggest all black women were Sapphire, Mammy or Jezebel, I'm not suggesting all black men wear one of the masks I'm about to describe. But when black men struggle with their black shadows, they often do fall into one of these categories.

The Player mask is a protective shield from feelings of male inadequacy and powerlessness. It is the boy shadow's attempt to collect on the debt he thinks the black woman owes him. While black women were learning not to expect to be cared for by black men, black men learned to expect to be cared for by black women and to have exceptions made for them because their male power had been rendered void under the dominant white male regime in America. The player usually keeps a stable of the same women around because his power comes from juggling them and having the control to keep them in the stable. With an "I am the man" attitude, he feels powerful being able to "hit it and quit it."

"I traveled a lot on my job and you best believe if I was in Cleveland I had a woman in Cleveland," Harry, a 38-year-old salesman, told me. "I might have a number at the hotel, but I got a girlfriend in Cleveland. But you also get tired of it because a lot of times you don't want to feel like that's all you have to bring to the table. You don't want to be looked at as a sexual object – a dog. My biggest thing is that I was that way and it's prevented me from having the type of family I would like to have."

The Player mask also keeps the boy-shadow at bay with adventure and hype.

CHAPTER 5 – SHADOW-BOXING WITH THE BOY

High on the false power of having multiple women, the black man has precious little time to think about feelings of male inadequacy. For some players, it's the number of women and not the sex that counts. Women are the trophy pieces he wins in his manhood battles with the boy shadow.

"I ain't gonna lie: I was a player," Jaimie, a 55-year-old musician, explained. "You told so many lies and put so many things in the game that you didn't know who you told what. To be honest with you, it's like you were a pool hustler. You played so many angles that you forgot what combination was the best combination. And then when it came back to you, you were standing there looking stupid. To save face, you had to move on. My maturity came when I got tired of playing. I knew this wasn't what it was supposed to be like. Who can I confide in? Who can I talk to? I can't talk to nobody."

Another way the Player mask attempts to pacify the boy shadow is by being a kind of sexual matador, pursuing and conquering women. Through sex, the boy shadow can feel like a man. Since sex is an entitlement of manhood, the pursuit of sex is, in fact, a way of rescuing himself whenever he feels inadequate, powerless or unmanly. The sexual matador is like a hunter who stalks his prey only when he's hungry for validation of his manhood or anxious that he isn't man enough and needs relief from those feelings.

For instance, when Derek, 48, a very successful business partner, came to therapy with his wife Angela, 46, a homemaker and volunteer at a local hospital, he had no idea what caused him to keep having affairs with white women. He always seemed to get caught. Derek was extremely anxious because Angela was threatening to leave for good this time, and she also promised to create a very big scandal since Derek's latest affair was with an employee.

Angela looked absolutely stunning in her latest guilt gift from Derek of a full-length raccoon coat. But it had not assuaged her fury this time. Derek kept promising never to cheat again, and he kept cheating. She felt betrayed and hurt, and wasn't willing to go through it one more time.

"I love my wife," Derek repeated over and over, looking bewildered and nervous. When I asked him why he kept having affairs, he looked confused. I helped him track the pattern to his affairs and it emerged that Derek sought extramarital sex whenever a major deal was about to happen or when he started to feel anxious about the success of the business. For him, the shadow of boy was certain to visit when he was at the height of success or something big was about to go down. Like stepping off a cliff, Derek would plunge to the bottom from his fear of success. Derek was afraid of losing his success because he still struggled with not being good enough as a black man. Not surprisingly, at these times, he tended to seek sex with white women.

In subsequent sessions, Derek learned to be aware when his black shadow started undermining his self-confidence. Instead of looking for validation and bolstering his manliness through sex with white women, he started talking to his wife and sharing his fears and feelings with her. Angela, who had often felt more like a trophy wife than a true friend and partner, was overjoyed to finally have an authentic connection with her husband and to be able to support him and feel his support for her.

Gregory was a black attorney hiding his black male inferiority complex behind the Player mask and also by using drugs to mask his real feelings. He had been in line to be a partner, but the pressure to compete with so many white colleagues made him feel like he would explode. He developed a cocaine habit and sexual addiction to escape from the stress and numb himself to the racism that was a part of his daily life at the all-white-but-him law firm. It was too hard to maintain the addictions and the job, and he was fired. His fiancé threatened to leave if he didn't get help, so he came to see me.

During a session with his fiancé, she admitted that she felt she barely knew him sometimes. He never talked to her about work or anything important in his life. "He prefers to talk to the janitor," she said.

"Well, he's a black man," Gregory explained. "We have a lot in common."

Gregory eventually admitted that he needed to get clean, and that he would probably do this best in a long-term treatment program. Before he left my office for the last time, I gently suggested that he consider the roles he'd taken as a reaction to the stress of slavery: the player and the addict. I told him I hoped his recovery program would give him space to examine the connection between the choices he'd made and the choices black men have been given for centuries by the dominant white, racist world. He promised he would think about it.

"Invincible Black Male" Mask

Some very successful black men wear what I call the Invincible Black Male mask. Although the men wearing these masks feel certain of their personal competence, they have repressed anger hidden behind the success label, which causes them to act out. They rage at society's injustice and mistreatment of them through destructive entitlement, engaging in reckless and often self-destructive behavior. Having been deprived of basic rights by the dominant society, they have unrealistic expectations of control and/or zest for danger and excitement.

Theodore was a supervisor in his predominantly white company. He had a high profile within his company as one of few minorities in a managerial position. He of course knew about the taboo against becoming sexually involved with his employees, yet he flirted with destruction by getting involved with white female employees. Over the years, he'd become more and more confident that he wouldn't get caught and took risks. He went out in public with his employee/lover of the moment, as if to dare anyone to accuse him of wrongdoing. Though his co-workers suspected, no one blew the whistle on his inappropriate and unethical behavior. In his mind, Theodore was the Invincible Black Male, a black man who had made it in the white world and was therefore exempt from the normal rules. He believed he had special powers that made him invincible in a way that other black men were not. But his predatory behavior toward white female employees was really just another way the shadow of the boy was acting out. Theodore wasn't having real, meaningful relationships; he was getting away with something, flouting the white establishment, proving that he could put one over on the white man.

When black Republican presidential candidate and business success Herman Cain suspended his campaign after several women accused him of sexual harassment, he looked smug in his Invincible Black Male mask. The feeling of having gotten away with something only increases this sense of special power. While they may feel powerful, it's a black shadow trap for these black men. They choose a self-destructive path in the quest to feel powerful under racism. In slavery, African American men and women were forced into inappropriate sexual relationships. Black men, like black women, were sexually exploited and abused. But the multigenerational legacy of slavery trauma passed on a pattern of inappropriate sex – including infidelity, incest and rape – to generations of black families.

"Bad Nigger" Mask

While some black men tend to act out against their internalization of the boy shadow by living on the edge and courting danger through destructive sexual encounters that can cost them their livelihoods, their families, their reputations and their health, other black males deal with their boy shadow by stepping into slavery's stereotype and wearing the Bad Nigger mask.

One of my clients, a 32-year-old Nate, felt defensive about how he was perceived. "You don't know me, but you're judging the book straight by the cover. 'Oh, he's a black man. Guard your wallet.' You come with good intentions, but they've already got you stereotyped. They look at us like such horrible creatures. And it really hurts me because we're some of the kindest people you could meet."

Nate had dropped out of an Ivy League school because he felt scrutinized and discriminated against. He ended up hanging out on the street corner, drinking with his friends. He became the bad nigger society expected all black men to be.

Nate came to see me because he was feeling discriminated against on the job and was depressed about where his life was when he knew he had been capable of so much more. He had begun to drink again, and he knew where this would lead, so he decided to face his demons rather than hide in a bottle.

"I think some black men switch over to that because that's what they expect of us," he told me. "So okay, you think I'm that in, so I'm a show you I can be that in. And you don't want to meet me. You don't want to mess with me. I've been there. I was rageful because that was the only power I had. I knew when I was acting like that bad nigger you wanted me to act like, I had your attention. But it was a double-edged sword: I got your attention but now I'm acting the way you expect me to act. At the time it didn't matter. All I had was my anger. That was the only weapon I had. I didn't have the job. I wasn't the manager. I couldn't tell you what to do, but you know what? I had my attitude, and I had your perception of me, and the fear I saw in your eyes when you thought I was the bad nigger. But I matured. It's less nerve wracking this way. And you're able to give more of yourself to the people who matter. And that definitely enhances your ego and gives you more confidence."

"Baby Man" Mask

Still other black men wear the Baby Man mask, turning their wives, girlfriends and lovers into adoring mothers to meet their feelings of adequacy in the role of son/lover. I'm not describing the Oedipal complex, when a son has sexual desire for his mother. This is about black men feeling most confident in the roles of son and lover. They know how to relate to their mothers and they feel adept in the mechanics of sex with their lovers.

Paradoxically, when the black woman expresses love and caring for her black man through indulgence – a mother's tolerance for her child – and pampering, it forces her to become more self-reliant and self-sufficient, which decreases her expectations of him as a man. This actually increases the anxiety he already feels about being man enough. It can also set up a destructive pattern, with each blaming the other because neither is living up to his or her authentic self in the relationship. Such a relationship lacks soul – the I and You – wholeness. It's more about two people playing roles than two people discovering their true inner beings together.

"Sugar Daddy" Mask

Black men who wear the Sugar Daddy mask find women who allow them to buy a feeling of manhood by providing material goods. The women stroke their egos and make them feel powerful, but it's not real. It's an economic transaction that carries no emotional truth. Like little boys seeking mother love and approval by bringing gifts that will result in a pat on the head and praise, sugar daddies need female adoration in order to feel manly. It is the balm on their wounded souls. But it's not the men these women adore, but the gifts they offer. The "boy" within might feel momentarily assuaged, but this is not a healthy, long-term solution for black men who yearn to feel wholeness and self-respect.

Wayne, a 36-year-old law school graduate who was working in the business world, became depressed after his girlfriend left him. He was on the verge of losing his job because he was staying at home rather than going to work. Wayne sat with his eyes stretched (as my mother would say), emanating unhappiness.

As I got to know him, I discovered that Wayne's feeling of inadequacy as a man was triggered in adolescence when he was diagnosed with epilepsy. He felt stigmatized and ashamed of his disease, believing it would lessen his chance of having a girlfriend. Naturally, Wayne's mother was very concerned about the seizures, but she overreacted by babying him, which made him feel even more defective and inadequate. The triple effects of society's view of black men as failures, the stigma of epilepsy, and his mother's babying him made Wayne's boy shadow strong. To compensate, he began spending his allowance on girls to try to impress them and win their affection, which made him feel manly.

Throughout his life, he'd established superficial relationships with women through the Sugar Daddy mask. He felt manhood fulfillment when a woman depended on him for material support. It made him feel that he had graduated from being the overprotected baby in his family to being a "real man." But his relationships with women never worked out. He longed for genuine love from a woman, but at the same time that he treated her like a paid prostitute. Wayne's relationships were like a rocky roller coaster ride with him feeling up and down, but mostly down all the time. Like many men I've worked with, Wayne wanted to feel manhood acceptance and approval from women, but he went about it the wrong way. He sought sex, comfort and admiration instead of mature, genuine relationships with women. In the end, these masks all cost black men, and they pay the price in self-worth and manhood identity.

Looking for Mrs. Self-Worth

"The media highlights the black athletes with the white girls. So you say to yourself, 'I want to get me a white girl because it seems like the money comes with the white woman'," said Rodney, who dated only white women.

The quest to own a white or near-white woman is often black men's attempt to appease the boy shadow. Some black men say they achieve more success in their careers when they have white or near-white women partners. It may even be true – they may raise their expectations of themselves and then credit the white women and not themselves for their success. They also might be so worried about white women's acceptance of them that they work harder at their jobs and in the relationship to prove that they are worthy of their white woman and to protect themselves from their partners' disapproval and rejection, which they fear.

For example, Larry, a well-established black surgeon who had been abusive to his black wife prior to their divorce, became the model mate with a white woman. Before the wedding, Larry bought his fiancé and her three children a house. He continued living in his own apartment until after the wedding out of respect for her white children. When the ex-wife and mother of his only biological child expressed anger and resentment on hearing this, his reaction was surprise and hurt. From his vantage point, he paid child support, which was what a responsible father did. Yes, he objected to his ex-wife's requests for additional money for extracurricular activities for their son, but that shouldn't have to be his responsibility, he told me. Larry didn't understand that the myth of black inferiority caused him to treat women differently because of their skin color. And he didn't understand how his relationships were ruled by the shadow boy. With his ex-wife, a black woman, he took out his anger and rage on her. With his white wife, he could only feel the illusion of manhood. It was an illusion because he needed to be with a white woman to feel it. In other words, he wasn't able to accept himself as a man in the world except when he was in relationship with the white object.

Another example of black men looking for Mrs. Self-Worth is the quest to win the prize of a light-skinned black woman. It's another way black men fool themselves into thinking they are more than just a worthless boy. All of black America, including mothers and sisters, share responsibility for this behavior. Black men act out the values inculcated in them by their families when they are "color struck."

"My father had a thing for light-skinned women. So I got me a redbone," confessed Amos, a 35-year-old participant in one of my workshops. A redbone is a black woman whose skin is so light that she blushes red. Amos went on to talk about his family. "One day, my son came home from kindergarten and he says, 'I don't like Ebony because she's dark.' I said, 'I thought she was your friend. And I thought she was real nice.' I think that's what my father lacked. That whole piece about skin color that was always unspoken is what influenced me the most."

Seeking refuge from the shadow of boy by choosing light-skinned sisters, brothers try to compensate for learned self-hate. Like black women, black men also define female beauty according to the dominant white culture's yardstick. It explains his longing to have a light-skinned black woman. But it's our black shadows acting on us, causing us to perpetuate racism within our own community and in our own intimate relationships. If a black man can't see the worth of a dark-skinned woman, how can he feel worthy in his own black skin? There's an unwholesome split that happens in his heart and mind when he chooses women based on their skin color.

Black Male Shame

"When I was 10 years old, I bought some candy from the neighborhood store," recounted 45-year-old Leroy. "The white owner didn't give me the correct change back. So I politely asked him for my correct change. I was proud of standing up for myself. Instead of giving me my change, he said I had the worst voice he had ever heard. He looked dead at me and asked, 'Boy, where did you get that terrible voice from?' I still feel like that boy: ashamed of being black and ashamed of not knowing how to talk. I learned to keep quiet, to go out of my way to avoid conflict."

The shame that dark-skinned Leroy felt at a tender young age was fed and nurtured by the skin color divisions in his own black community. He became a successful man and was thrilled when a light-skinned black woman named Jacqueline expressed an interest in him. Cream in his coffee, he used to say proudly. For a time, he felt that he was finished with the black male inferiority complex that had plagued him since childhood. Jacqueline made him feel special. When he was with her, he was accepted into social circles that were reserved for light-skinned black folks. That, in and of itself, inflated his ego, giving him a sense of importance.

Over time, Leroy made some poor business decisions that landed him in deep financial trouble. Not wanting Jacqueline (now his wife) to be disappointed in him, and because he was afraid of conflict, he didn't tell her. Instead of taking action to clean up his financial mess and salvage what remained, he was passive and did nothing. The boy in him hoped he could escape feeling powerless and helpless by avoiding conflict. He equated conflict with the boy who couldn't win against the racist store owner. As a result, he lost his business and Jacqueline left him. He ended up feeling more like the boy than before.

Leroy had been shadow-boxing with the boy for a very long time when he walked into my office. And he was very tired. He was filled with self-hate and pain. I was impressed that he had come to therapy, and could see it had taken tremendous effort. Investing in himself (which is what therapy is) was his first act toward self-acceptance and realness – authenticity. It paid off. Leroy learned to handle both conflict and the black shadow for which he now has a name.

Slavery and the Black Male Psyche

Missing out on nurturance as a boy, and later the security of an intimate relationship with a mate, black male existence in slavery was lonely and scary. At the whim of slave masters and white overseers, black men could be maimed, severely beaten or killed at any time. Out of slavery, the continuance of racism contributed to the maintenance of adaptive strategies needed to endure the life-altering experience of the black man. Knowing his only purpose was working and breeding with black slave women to produce slave children to increase the white master's wealth, black men became uncomfortable around black women. Given the job of breeding children who would not belong to their mothers or fathers, he knew that his involvement with her was another assault on her mind, body and spirit. Unable to spare the woman or himself from the depersonalization of slavery, he disconnected from both himself and black women. In the company of black women, he felt like the "boy stud" slavery had turned him into, not the man warrior from his tribe in Africa.

Psychologically exiled from himself, he shut off his tender feelings and genuine emotions, or masked them, and allowed his body to do what was required. The long-term legacy of this situation is that black men today suffer from manhood insecurity, which draws them toward sex with women but keeps them from being genuine and vulnerable with them, or making a commitment to them. Handcuffed to the boy shadow, black men often find themselves wearing one of the many masks they use to disguise feelings of manhood impotence and fear of rejection.

Feeling terribly self-conscious about others' perception of him, the black male engages in denial, projection, and mistrust of himself and women. He attacks, finding fault with black women before they find fault with him. Or he makes them surrogate mothers in his search for unconditional love. He tries to resist the white man's image of him by taking his white woman. He denies manhood insecurity by fathering children that he has no commitment to raising and at the same time wishing for respect. He projects his paralysis onto black women, seeing them as the cause of his failure and agents of his defeat.

Many black men experience a contradiction of needs: they want to be in charge and powerful, but seek safety and protection in a woman. They want love, but withdraw from closeness by spending more time with the boys or by having more than one woman. He wants a rich family life, but risks it or abandons it for sex. He wants respect, but has little for himself. He wants educational success, but fears intellectual failure. He wants to be a man, but can't look at the boy in the mirror because he will see the dreaded image left over from slavery: the "nigger."

Living in an atmosphere chronically charged with racial tension is frustrating and anxiety provoking. African American men cover up their nervousness through withdrawal, detachment and procrastination. Afraid of trusting anyone (himself included), he avoids contact when possible or limits his interaction with others, including significant others. Nervous of failing and of not being accepted, he procrastinates. Procrastination is what often keeps him from feeling successful in his intimate relationships. But rather than take responsibility for it, he lashes out at his woman. "If you don't want to wait for me to do it, do it yourself." Or, "You can't never please no black woman." In the meantime, his inner dialogue goes something like this: "A white woman knows how to treat a man. My wife would probably be happier with a white man. She probably thinks I'm a no-good black man."

A black man's estrangement from self, women and family leaves him out in the cold. His sense of not belonging to anyone or anywhere comes from not having an authentic self. Feelings of guilt, anger and self-rejection leave him wrestling with his boy shadow and losing. Finding his way back home is not as easy as clicking his heels three times. Understanding the black shadow and accepting responsibility for it is what is required for him to reclaim his seat in the family as husband and father. Only then will he find peace of mind, body, and soul that will give him unconditional self-love and allow him to be the man he wants to be.

In the transfixed state of boy, black men won't stop such destructive behaviors as fathering fatherless children, killing and dying for so-called "respect" and claiming to be naturally polygamous. Such behaviors are no more than trade-offs for the appearance of manhood. Authentic relationships, the ability to delay gratification, having an internal sense of status, and the ability to be vulnerable are the conscious markings of a real man. Achieving peace of mind instead of sacrificing it for temporary pleasures is an act of self-love and the enlightenment of manhood.

Letting Go

There are many black men who refuse to follow slavery's dictates and who refuse to wear the limited masks that have been assigned to black men since slavery. But it's hard to find one's authentic self in the onslaught of negative images, role models and lies about black inferiority. We should not expect perfection, but nurture black men's willingness to commit, to be faithful and loving. As black men come to define for themselves what their ideal self is made of – not just farming themselves out as studs – the whole community will greet them with joy.

There are so many examples of black men who have made this journey successfully. One example close to my heart is Melvin. A retired accountant, he grew up learning about manhood from his mother's religious and life teachings and his father's example – both the good and the bad. Melvin painfully admits that between the ages of 18 and 20, he played the role of stud, having one-night stands with many girls in college. "I took on the role of player because the girl I was in love with ended our relationship and I gave up on relationships. I wanted no feelings involved and no expectations."

It was while at home on a school break that he had an "Aha!" moment. He looked at his mother and sisters and realized his player behavior was deeply disrespectful to women. "I went back and apologized to all those women that I ran into again," he remembers, "but I couldn't apologize to all of them because I never bothered to get contact information for many of my one-night stands."

A year later, Melvin met Valerie. They became friends first because Melvin wanted to take his time. He wouldn't even sleep with her until they became engaged eight months later. Melvin married Valerie and stayed married for 35 years until she died of heart disease.

He says he made a choice about his manhood. "It was important to support my wife and take care of my family. I didn't cheat because I considered the relationship sacred. I really committed and decided to follow my own path, not to follow the path of friends who bought lifetime memberships in the players club. The only legacy that I care to leave from my life on Earth, is for God to say 'Well done, my good and faithful servant.' That means being the best friend, father, husband and overall person that I can be in this life."

Self-validation is possible without bargaining with the boy shadow. Self-discovery from facing the shadow instead of trying to out-box it can reignite the burned out flame of the soul, freeing the man. But here's the catch: black men have to be willing to lose their cool and be emotional. And I don't just mean angry – I mean the full range of emotions that human beings need to express to heal and achieve wholeness.

"One of the things we're not talking about as black men is how we're socialized," 39-year-old Charles told me. "We're socialized to be these tough exterior people. I'm an extremely sensitive guy, and I was always straddling the fence trying to figure out where I was. And it took me a long time to realize wherever you are, you have to be who you are."

Real manhood means being able to tolerate vulnerability. It is the shadow of boy that fears vulnerability. Black men will not stop doubting themselves and being frightened of their genuine feelings, impulses and desires if they don't allow themselves to be vulnerable. Of course we know why it's so hard. In slavery, a black man could not afford to show vulnerability or he would die. And in the patriarchy, which affects men of all colors, the ideal of manhood eschews emotionality and vulnerability. Nevertheless, real men do cry. And real men need to trust themselves with emotions.

Black men must learn to hold conversations with themselves and the black shadow to avoid a hostile take-over by the boy. Just as you learned to make friends with your enemies in childhood, you must do so with the black shadow. You can't let it rule your life, but you can't ignore it, either. Try to transform it from being your enemy to being a reminder that you have work to do to eradicate the belief in black inferiority.

Many black men walk around feeling like badness itself. Feeling vulnerable and untrustworthy, too many succumb to the pressures, becoming monsters straight from the swamps of racism. As monsters, they physically, sexually and emotionally abuse the women and children in their lives.

CHAPTER 5 – SHADOW-BOXING WITH THE BOY

Gary's Story

On a cold, icy Sunday afternoon in 1993, the black shadow that my 20-year-old nephew Gary had been boxing with met him head on. That day, the city of Philadelphia was paralyzed by a blizzard. It was my mother who delivered the news to me: Gary was in hiding after shooting his girlfriend in a domestic dispute.

Ever since he'd crossed over into the drug life, Gary's mom had been expecting the dreaded call telling her he was dead, but she never expected this. I rushed over to her house and found my sister staring out a window and rocking back and forth as if she was soothing her own inner child.

"I can't do anything. No one can help Gary now," she said bleakly.

It turned out she was wrong. One person could help Gary, and that was Gary, himself.

Gary's story is a familiar melody in the black song of life. He was a promising young black man with a loving family who made bad choices. He ended up doing drugs and nearly murdering the mother of his child. During those years, he was lost to us. His black shadow ruled him, and he was eaten up inside with self-hate and the need to do self-destructive acts. It led to that terrible night when he shot his girlfriend, followed by five years of prison and pain for himself and all of us who love him.

The way we learn to overcome self-hate is a process. In Gary's case, it began with a major event to shake him out of the unhealthy status quo he'd created.

"I began teetering with the idea of coming back to being a responsible member of society after I shot Keisha," Gary told me years later. "I realized what I did was wrong. And she didn't deserve it. Nobody deserves to be shot. But I was just teetering with the idea." Then Gary was put in solitary confinement for fighting with another inmate over a honey bun.

"I was so ashamed," he admitted. "I didn't want to call home and say, 'I'm at it again. After all this, I'm acting the fool again.' And then I received a letter from Mom. She didn't really say how bad she was hurt, but it was there between every line. I kept seeing the invisible words: 'No matter how hard we try, you just don't want to get yourself together.' I was in a single cell when I was in the hole, and all I had was that letter. And it tore me up."

Recognizing the impact his actions had on his loved ones was the catalyst for Gary to start thinking about a different future for himself. "Mom talked about my daughter needing a father, so I said to myself, 'Man, when I get out of here I'm going down to the education building and I'm going to get my GED.'"

While he was in prison, Gary participated in group therapy. It was there that he started to understand that he'd made bad choices in the past out of a deep sense of self-hate. He faced his black shadow and saw how it had been leading him into trouble. Empowered with this new self-knowledge, he went back to school and studied hard. He passed the GED test on his first try, earning the third highest score in the prison. "People were telling me I could be a first-level college student," Gary recalled. "I started taking more classes."

But once Gary set himself on this new path, he ran up against resistance within the culture of the prison. "You're ostracized for not being a part of the 'nigger this,' 'nigger that,' prison life," he told me. "You clearly have to choose. You can't just teeter. I was ridiculed. I was scorned. Guys would say, 'You always in a book.' So they stopped coming by my cell. Guys stopped working out with me, saying, 'You'll probably be reading this weekend.' They would ask me why I wanted to go to the library to read when I could be playing cards, or why a nigger like me was working in the computer lab. It got to be a joke to them. One guy in particular would laugh and say, 'Come on out the white house,' every time he saw me in the education building.' His other favorite thing to say was, 'If they let a nigger like you in there it must be easy.'"

Gary had tried to avoid being rejected by other young black men when he was in high school. To prove he was one of them, he dropped out and became a hoodlum. But this time he was older, and he stayed the course and let them call him a "sell-out."

As Gary confronted his own black shadow, he learned to look at himself honestly and not judge others. "It's a thin line that separates you from them," he said, referring to his former friends who now shunned him. "You are aware of the fact that they are degrading themselves or degrading their people and whatnot, but it's just one flip side of you. I just flipped sides. Now I realize that it's not good to go around calling each other niggers. And it's not alright for me to walk around calling women bitches."

Why do some young black men choose a path of self-destruction? Why did Gary?

"You think you're nothing, and the next man is basically less than you," he explained. "If you think you're nothing, it's not a hard skip to think that people are even less than that. It's nothing at stake."

It was in prison where Gary learned to appreciate the good in himself and to find it in others. "I was thinking about what made me start to believe I was something. When I came to prison, I met people that were good people. I was well liked. I've met criminals that were genuinely good guys. Not just good guys, but guys that were smart. They would tell me that they saw those things in me. I was lucky enough to come by my computer teacher. He took a liking to me. Some people in the situation that we're in are not liked simply by the way they look. I made a choice that I was going to do my best to get my life together, to make something of myself. And once I did that, I started to see what all the people saw in me. Once I started acting on some of those things that people kept saying I'm good at, I started doing good at it."

Gary also started to realize the value of talking openly and honestly about his feelings as a way to take power from the black shadow. He learned to share himself with his family and friends, and he was surprised and gratified by how much love and support there was for him. The day he told us about his guilt at his step-brother's death – Gary had asked him to go out and get something, and that's when the young man was shot – we all better understood what had driven him to choose the self-destructive path he'd taken soon after. And Gary learned that he'd drawn faulty conclusions about himself out of his own guilt, shame, anger and silence.

"After he was shot, I was like who cares. I didn't think I'd make it to 25. I was happy, even in jail, to turn 25. I was happy just to be alive. I'm 25, I'm alive. And the things we were doing, I should be dead. I'm getting ready to be 26, I have a beautiful daughter, I have a wonderful family, I'm doing wonderful. Life is good."

Many black men suffer from hopelessness having developed the dangerous attitude: "Why bother." What black men need most is to find their way to authentic manhood by putting the boy to rest and challenging the black shadows within. When they can take a steady, unafraid look at their wounded souls, they will finally find self-understanding, forgiveness and healing.

Exercises for Black Men

To create change, you have to commit to working on yourself. Here are 6 steps to creating positive change in your life. (You may want to get a notebook or journal to write in, or open up a new computer file and name it "I Challenge My Black Shadow.")

Step 1: *Get Your Mind in Shape.* Just like a good workout regimen builds muscles, mental exercises will help you become the man you want to be, free of the black shadow. Go to a quiet place and visualize positive black male identity. Make a list of adjectives that describe positive black male identity. Make a list of values, behaviors and expectations you have for positive black male identity. Assess how close or far you are on each item. Set specific goals for meeting your objectives. Commit to an action plan. Review it weekly or monthly.

Step 2: *Player Suspension.* If you identified with the Player description, try to stop your pattern of behavior by being involved with one woman only for four weeks. Pay attention to positive and negative feelings. It helps to write in a journal every day so you can hear yourself. What makes you feel anxious and how do you manage your anxiety? What was happening inside of you when you wanted to be with someone else? What was happening between you and the woman you were with?

Step 3: *Self-Inventory.* Identify at least five things you're proud of and five things you're ashamed of. Identify five fears and five things you want to accomplish. And then every day for the next five days, answer one of the following questions and use your answers to develop a personal action plan.

- ■ **Who Are You?** How do you define yourself as a black male? What qualities do you like best about yourself? What qualities do you like least? What are the opposite qualities of those you like least about yourself? How would you integrate these qualities into your life?

- **Do You Like You?** What does being a black man mean in your life? What do you get criticized for, whether true or not? What do you find yourself being most defensive about? What are the undeveloped parts of your life?

- **Who Do You Judge?** What kind of black man do you hold in contempt? What do you dislike in him? What is your relationship to that quality in yourself? Who is a male in your life with whom you have an emotionally charged relationship? What characteristic would you like to change in this person? What is the meaning of this characteristic in you?

- **Who Do You Blame?** Who do you blame for your problems in life? How might you be responsible? What is your role in organizing (provoking, condoning, facilitating, or discouraging) the other person's behavior?

- **Who Do You Want to Become?** How does the "nigger" or boy character influence your life? Who does it blame? Who does it protect? How do male relatives think about the "nigger" or boy character? What are the ways in which you might re-orient your psyche to respect black males? What would genuine self-acceptance mean to your life?

Step 4: *Replace Negative Thinking.* Ask yourself what you believe in your heart of hearts that you'll never be able to achieve because you're a black man, and then write yourself a positive affirmation for achieving it. For example, if you believe you won't find love and happiness, write, "I radiate love and happiness." Affirmations are positive declarative statements about your desired situation that you repeat daily in order to make them real in your mind and possible.

Step 5: *Brotherhood.* Invite a male friend or a group of male friends to meet with you weekly or monthly to talk about personal feelings and black male identity. Agree to hold each other accountable (i.e. hold him to player suspension). Set ground rules for honesty, respect, confidentiality, agreeing to disagree and taking turns to set the agenda. Topics might include:

- What makes black men good partners?
- What do black men contribute to the rift between black men and women?
- What would make black men want to commit to a relationship with a black woman?
- What do black men secretly fear?
- What are signs of black male self-rejection?
- What makes black men good fathers?
- What do black men feel about their sexual objectification?

Step 6: *Fathers/Sons Rap.* If you are a father, talk openly to your son(s) individually and/or in groups about race and how it makes you feel, and find out how it makes them feel. Talk about the myth of black inferiority. Read and discuss books on black history. Visit places and events to increase knowledge of black history.

Chapter 6
Casting the Shadow Over Intimacy

Even though today's African Americans were never slaves, we each inherited the multigenerational legacy of slavery trauma. I realize this is a much-debated point in the black community, but if you've read all the way to Chapter 6, then I think you get my point about the importance of accepting the truth about the residual impact of slavery on African Americans. We're still controlled by the myth of black inferiority and still intimidated and kept in check by our fears of the "nigger" stereotype. What does it mean to inherit the legacy of slavery trauma? First you have to understand what psychological trauma is. In a nutshell, it occurs when someone suffers intolerable fear in response to an overwhelming and life-threatening event. It's no stretch of the imagination to realize that black slaves were psychologically traumatized by slavery. And since slavery gave way to racism, every generation of African Americans since emancipation has had to grapple with ongoing psychological trauma around racism and the events of slavery.

In more concrete terms, the trauma of slavery that we carry induces fear, shame and anger in us. Trauma survivors typically react fearfully when they come into contact with people, places or things that remind them of the original traumatic experience. In this chapter, as we examine our heterosexual black relationships, I am suggesting that our intimate, adult relationships activate those traumatic reminders about slavery. Specifically, they recall slavery's brutal enforcement of the stud-breeder roles for black men and women.

White masters forced black women and black men to "breed" during slavery. Black men were forced to have sex with women whether they were willing or not. And black women were forced to submit. On an unconscious level, our black shadows remember these roles, and so when we get together, feelings of shame, blame and fear can be triggered. In the crucible of the black heterosexual relationship, intense fear of one another and learned distrust are aspects of our reactions to the legacy of slave trauma we carry. We might even come up with unconscious strategies to avoid one another and sabotage our relationships in order to protect ourselves from reliving the trauma of slavery.

Black men and women are not living the way we were meant to live. We've gotten tangled up in the lies of slavery and black inferiority. Our racial memory of slavery and the instructions we were given to become "nigger" in order to stay alive takes the black man and black woman away from his/her true self. We're not true to our own intelligence, spirit, strength and character because we have that loud voice in our heads criticizing us and knocking us down all the time. So when I talk about the difficulties we have in our relationships, I am not implying that all black relationships are broken or inferior. Rather, I'm asking all of us to examine our relationships and ask ourselves, "Am I reenacting the habits, patterns or lessons from slavery in my relationship?" The statistics on black marriages and single parent households reflect a pattern of fracture in our relationships that, to me, is reminiscent of what happened to black relationships under slavery. I'm suggesting that we all cultivate black shadow awareness so we can stop letting the black shadow tell us who we can be in our relationships. Our true selves will become clear only when we stop believing in the lie of black inferiority and start connecting to our soulful nature.

As victims of post-slavery traumatic stress, black men and women have markedly diminished participation in family life, as evidenced by the troubling statistics on black marriages and single-parent households. We may experience intense psychological distress when we're around one another because the "other" symbolizes the slavery experience. We might have feelings of detachment from one another, as reflected in the battle between the sexes. Or, we might find ourselves taking a super critical stance about the faults of the other. Other symptoms of post-slavery traumatic stress include difficulty committing to each other; suspiciousness and mistrust on the part of black women, who believe they can't rely on black men to be there for them; dread on the part of black men that they will not be able to take care of their women and children, as was true during slavery. We also might have a sense of a foreshortened future, which manifests in our expectations that we won't be getting married and raising our children in a two-parent household.

For any victim of post-traumatic stress, if the original traumatizing event is

CHAPTER 6 – CASTING THE SHADOW OVER INTIMACY

not named and examined, it's not possible to break its destructive hold on the psyche. It's not possible to integrate the experience into the conscious mind and understand it. Instead, it can haunt us and our children and grandchildren far into the future. It seems crazy to me that slavery has not been specifically named as the traumatic event affecting black men and women today. It is so clear to me that it's the key to understanding our behaviors, and the most accurate way to diagnose and treat black family dysfunctions.

There are a number of factors that have left African Americans in a state of black shock, which presents as relationship failure, fractured families, addictions, violence and more. These factors include: the overwhelming life event of slavery and continuous racism; emotional shut-down; unconscious and conscious acceptance of the myth of black inferiority; self-hate; and group disharmony as a result of all of the items above. Because we're just beginning to come out of our collective denial that slavery has an impact on us, we're barely aware of how slavery relates to our conflicted feelings and self-hating behaviors. We reenact the trauma instead of facing it and healing from it. Those reenactments include staying single, having babies out of wedlock, teenage pregnancy, absentee fathers and single mothers. In the highly charged relationship between black men and women, images of the stud and breeder come to life followed by fears of rejection, abandonment and loss.

Sure, all of us know that slavery happened. But most of us have no awareness of its long-term impact on us. It's not uncommon for trauma survivors to develop amnesia, to repress the memory of the event or to repress the feelings associated with the event. I would argue that we have black amnesia. We have repressed our feelings associated with slavery. Therefore, we have no understanding of the black shadow that poisons the relationships between African American men and women. The memory of feeling like the "nigger" slave man and woman lives in our unconscious minds even though it is disowned in the conscious mind.

Adults who have had traumatic family experiences tend to be anxious in relationships, resulting in anxious closeness or anxious distance between the partners. The closeness or distance is a defensive reaction against memories of abandonment as a child. In this same trauma process, black men and women develop anxious relationships – mostly anxious distance — as a defense against the memories of abandonment, shame and betrayal in slavery. Their anxious distance is reflected in the black woman's proud stance as the strong black woman or "Mammy" and the black man's proud stance as the "Player." To protect against the slave woman's memory of feeling alone and helpless, the black woman uses the Mammy mask to cover up her anxiety. To protect against the slave man's memory of being powerless and unable to provide for the black woman, the black man uses the Player mask to hide his anxiety. The black woman over-functions in the relationship and rages ("I don't need no man") at him while he under-functions in the relationship and rages ("You ain't the only woman") at her.

Fallout from the Breeder-Stud Relationship

The system of slavery deliberately drove black men and women apart and took from them any larger purpose for existing as a couple other than to produce more workers for the economic benefit of white families. The enforced breeder-stud relationship between black men and women was one of the most destabilizing events in the family history of African Americans, kicking off dysfunctional couple dynamics that, in turn, redirect our attention away from the mutual need of black men and women to counter and resist racism.

"A slave girl was expected to have children as soon as she became a woman," recounted former slave Hillary Yellerday in a book of oral histories called *Bullwhip Days* by James Mellon. Some slave girls bore children at the age of 12 and 13 years old, fathered by grown black men. Instead of black girls being treasured, protected and prepared for marriage, they were raped and forced to breed without gentleness, without the consideration and ceremony that had been associated with their passage from childhood to womanhood in their African tribes. The formation of a family through marriage and then the birth of children was denied to black women and men by the new white owners. It was slavery that forced the black woman to let her body be used by multiple men and have children out of wedlock with uncommitted men. But black women ignore the root and instead put the blame on "irresponsible" black men.

Likewise, black boys were denied the rites of passage from childhood to adulthood. Not allowed to engage in the act of courting and marriage that symbolized adult responsibility in Africa, black men in America were forced to appear immature and irresponsible. Slavery forced black men to be forever "boy," and it is that shame and pain that they are still dealing with today. But they ignore the root and blame the problem on "angry" (emasculating) black women. We aren't seeing how the traumatic legacy of slavery is affecting how we treat one another and how we see one another. We don't connect this legacy to the problems we today have as unmarried mothers, rolling stone fathers and wounded singles.

The white men who sexually exploited and assaulted black women, and their white female counterparts who silently colluded, later reframed the situation to cast themselves as blameless by classifying black women as sexually depraved, promiscuous and morally loose (summed up by the Jezebel). This is a racist stereotype from which black women have yet to escape. This story began almost as soon as black women were brought to America naked and in shackles, and has been repeated so often that we African Americans believe it's true. When we complain about the problem of black teenage pregnancy and multiple out-of-wedlock births, we're echoing the racist idea that black women are basically sluts.

The black man's story as told by white America is that he is the dog who handles his business with whatever "bitch" is in heat and then wanders away when he's finished. The fundamental dynamic of white supremacy is that it relies on disharmony and failed relationships between black men and women. The white world profits from our failure to form stable and loving relationships. We are so busy fighting each other that we're not putting our energies into rising up from the bottom. We're less of a threat – less able to compete with whites – when we're divided. With historical knowledge and psychological understanding, black men and women can start to remember that it was slavery that infected us with dysfunctional and destructive behaviors. We can find the energy and optimism to reclaim our rightful relationships and create healthy bonds of love and commitment. It's up to us to make this happen. We must resist the black shadow when it tries to insert a wedge between us, driving us farther apart with suspicion and stereotypes that come directly from slavery.

Sex as a Measure of Black Relationship Health

Black slaves were not allowed to own their own bodies. Their white masters owned their bodies and decided who would have sexual access and when and how often. The breeder-stud relationship was the only sanctioned relationship between opposite-sex slaves. Sexual relationships were equated with conflict and humiliation, but sex was the driving force in black male-female relationships rather than love, affection, connection, mutual respect, shared values and shared pursuits. I believe sex is still, far too often, the driving force in black male-female relationships today. When the focus is on sex, the breeder-stud ghosts of slavery overshadow our relationships so that we can't focus our energy on forging long-lasting, harmonious relationships.

A large percentage of couples who seek therapy are having problems in the bedroom, and in my practice I see many of these couples. Al and Gloria came to therapy because Gloria wasn't interested in sex and Al wanted me to fix this. Al was a physician and Gloria was a stay-at-home mother. They lived in their dream house and had three children, all of whom were doing well in school. Gloria's mother lived with them and helped out with the kids. Al thought he was the model provider, and he couldn't understand Gloria's lack of interest in sex.

I interviewed them about the history of their relationships and it was revealed by Gloria that Al had had several affairs over the course of their 15-year marriage. Although Gloria was able to buy anything she wanted, she felt powerless in the relationship. She couldn't stop Al from having affairs. In fact, one affair had produced a child, and Gloria had to live with the fact that Al was a father to another woman's child. She felt like she couldn't complain because Al was a responsible father to their children and a good provider and she didn't want to disrupt her children's lives with divorce. Gloria's lack of interest in sex was very much related to her feelings of powerlessness in the marriage. Saying no to sex felt like the only thing she had any control over.

I have come to understand that when one partner loses interest in sex, it doesn't mean that sex is no longer the driving energy of the relationship. The couple's focus is still on sex, although now they're fighting about sex instead of having it. Many of the black women who've come to see me because of low sex drive have had unfaithful or unhelpful partners, which activates more slavery trauma. They feel they are being used for sex and then abandoned. Low sex drive is their way of saying, "Hell no!"

A black woman has to understand how the black shadow is sabotaging her expectations. It's telling her that a black man will never take care of her because she's not worthy, and black men are untrustworthy. She tells herself she can take care of herself and the people around her. She stops expecting him to come through for her, but she still feels anger, resentment, disappointment and hurt. Instead of telling her partner what she needs and putting her feelings into words, she withholds sex.

The men in these couples are often good providers. They work long hours and pay all the bills and felt they were doing their job, living up to their part of the marital contract. They defined that marital contract as including the option of not being involved in household activities. In exchange for their hard work and material support, they expect their wives to be sexually available whenever they want sex.

From the time that black women were captured and kidnapped to be slaves, they became the sexual property of white men and had to be sexually available to their owners and overseers at any time, and to any black man that the white man wanted to breed her with. Black women still carry that shame, humiliation, disrespect, and devaluation of being sexually objectified. It's no mystery why a black woman might feel little or no sexual desire when in a situation that brings up these feelings and triggers the legacy of slavery trauma in her. The female spirit has no desire to submit to the auction block, where black women were priced for their breasts, eyes, teeth, and potential for work and breeding.

It's not always women who withhold sex in relationships. When men come to therapy to work on the embarrassing situation of low sex drive or performance issues, they usually discover that they aren't feeling seen and valued for their soul, just their stud services and paychecks. They're often confused about sex. On the one hand, they are supposed to be built for it – all the stereotypes of the "nigger" black man refer to his big balls – yet their black shadow reminds them all the time that they'll never be more than "boy." The internalization of the stud stereotype is both a source of shame and pride, accounting for black men's confused self-concept.

Contemporary black couples don't think consciously about the breeder-stud roles or the legacy of slavery trauma in their lives. All they want is to have their unnamed longings for connection, love, manhood and womanhood be fulfilled. In mid-life and later, couples settle for mediocre connections and swallow their bewilderment and disappointment. Always lurking in the shadow is the belief in black inferiority – their own and their partner's. I have even heard couples say that whites have better relationships than blacks. With men and women blaming each other for the failures in their relationships, we miss an opportunity to work together to see the root cause – the primary wound – which is slavery.

The Black Queen Looking for Her King

A black woman's spirit yearns for a partner who sees her beauty and treasures her for her whole Being, like she imagines an African king cherishes and honors his queen. The task for black women is to believe we are queens, and stop secretly viewing ourselves as the "niggers" of slavery. The black shadow brainwashes us into believing we're the lowest of the low – unworthy maids, servants, slaves, "ho's," sexually promiscuous freaks. The Mammy mask of strong black woman sets up our expectation that black women should shoulder the burden and responsibility for intimacy and affection with little or no attention to our needs for tenderness and emotional care. Just thinking about that makes me want to give a soul-deep scream of protest all the way back to the time of slavery. Black women should expect *more*, not less, from black men, and we should accept no less.

We shield ourselves from pain by refusing to make ourselves vulnerable to black men, expecting (and receiving) rejection or sexual objectification. We must learn to be open to connection and interdependence. We must reclaim our beauty and our bodies and our authentic sexuality in relationships. Everything I've asked you to do so far in this book has been hard, but this might be the hardest of all, because it will require a leap of faith in yourself and in black men. We've been taught to regard with skepticism their capacity to come through for us and truly love us. We will have to reach past our fears and doubts and take risks.

The bottom line is that black relationships are too centered around sex, whether it is the female who denies her sexuality or the male who's got to have it. Sex is the number one reason that black men give for cheating on the women whom they purport to love. For women, it is one of the primary reasons we give for staying in bad relationships. When a black woman laments the absence of a man in her life and talks about being lonely, she is really talking about sex. Sex is also the motive for women to willingly man-share – mistresses, one-night stands. They settle for second string instead of waiting to be someone's one and only. Young black men and women view sex as the one and only tie that binds them in relationship. They don't know to look for and create true intimacy. The soaring statistics on AIDS in the black community would suggest that sex is more important to us than our own longevity.

Frankly, sex is the weakest link in a relationship. No matter how good it is in the beginning, it's not the sole or most important tie that binds people in long-lasting, mutually satisfying and mutually supportive intimate relationships. When we focus all our relationship energy on sex, we neglect our needs for trust, commitment, respect and loyalty.

The Black Couple's Dance of Intimacy

If we could choreograph a silent scene showing a black couple's intimacy, we would have a black man running away from the black woman whom he just can't seem to please, and the black woman stuck in the martyr position, doing for herself and everyone around her – as usual – because she can never count on a black man to step up and stick around. They would both display mistrust and disappointment in the other. The black man thinks he is running away from the black woman's sharp tongue and anger, but the disapproval he sees in her eyes only mirrors the way he feels about himself. She, on the other hand, thinks she is being strong but the rejection she sees in his eyes are a mirror of her own feelings of ugliness because she is black and therefore not worthy of being cared for the way she imagines white women are cared for by their men.

President Barack Obama and First Lady Michelle Obama defy the above image of the black couple. But before we had Barack and Michelle, many of us didn't have this kind of positive role modeling simply because of the poor statistics on black relationships and the dearth of positive black couples in the media. The above visual of the couple running from each other depicts the black man and woman letting slavery and racism define them. Their interlocking fears, which are manifested in their dance of intimacy, turn into bitter projections against the other: The black woman projects her sense of feminine failure and devaluation onto the black man, who projects his sense of inadequacy and manhood failure onto the black woman. It becomes a circular destructive pattern, like a wheel that just keeps on spinning. Both are caught in the spokes of slavery and each is moving to the beat of the black shadow that keeps on playing that old sad song. But neither can face their black shadows because they are focused on their anger at the other. Leroy, the black man who married a light-skinned woman (I discussed him in the previous chapter) painfully admitted that his wife told him, "I should have married a white man," when she walked out on him. Even though he was struggling with his boy shadow, he confessed that he wondered if a white woman would have been more understanding.

Chained together in the rhythm of slavery, with each pointing the finger at the other, accusations fly. The black man accuses the black woman of not knowing how to treat black men. Some black men have taken it a step further saying, "White women know how to be submissive and black women don't." The black shadow implication is that if a black woman returned to the submissiveness she endured in slavery, she would be more desirable as a partner. The battle cry of the black woman is that black men can't be counted on. Some women have also taken it to the next level, saying, "White men might not want to, but they take care of home." The assumption is that black men will never be as good as white men.

The overwhelming majority of African Americans treat the battle cry of black men and women as the beginning, middle and end of the story of black heterosexual relationships. Most of us don't bother to put it in historical context, nor do we examine the slave shadows that intrude on our black relationships. Somewhere at sea during the long voyage from Africa to the New World, we lost our ability to be beloveds. We were turned into "niggers" on the shores of white America. Our spirits long to separate the beloved from "nigger" and reclaim black manhood and womanhood.

The finger-pointing and complaints between the sexes weigh the black community down. We become veiled sport for the *People* magazine polls, demographers and the like who declare: "The institution of marriage is dead in the black community."

"Educated black women over 40 have a better chance of being struck by lightning than of getting married."

"Young black men see fathering children as jewels in their crown."

"The black family is matriarchal."

"Black men are absentee fathers."

The stress on black love is slavery. The black man was made weak and powerless before the black woman, who was made a sex object and super strong before the black man. These roles are not the truth. We know that our full humanity is far more complex and far more nuanced, but we haven't been allowed to express and live our full humanity – not under slavery, and not under racism. Both the black man and the black woman were objectified in slavery. Each was property, unable to protect self or other, unable to marry or love freely, and unable to make family commitments. Slavery passed on to freed black women and men the unresolved shame of lost dignity and enforced breeder-stud roles, and the continued loss of our sense of entitlement to nurture and explore our full humanity.

In the racist aftermath of slavery, black men and women struggled to overcome unimaginable horrors such as segregation, lynchings, systematic discrimination, daily humiliation and more, and our internalized shame and belief in black inferiority led to self-fulfilling prophecies of the black man as unreliable and the black woman as controlling. We need to reexamine the survival mechanisms that were useful in slavery but that now make us stagnant and pathological. We need to challenge the disconnection between the physical and psychological aspects of black men and women. We need to challenge the black shadow.

The Black Couple's Shame

The black man's inability to protect and provide for his woman and children was a great source of shame for him during slavery, and it still is for many men. Shame is a very complex emotion that often leads to denial. Denial by way of projection onto black women helps black men to guard against their internalization of powerlessness and the view that it's a defect in their character structure. It's the black woman's fault, not his. Thus he can avoid the feeling of shame that he'll never be a white man.

Black men assume that black women have the power that eludes them, and black women assume that black men have unused power. Each maintains a false belief that the other is holding out on him or her. The truth that matters is that each is holding out on the self while waiting for the other to make it right. In the meantime, the entire black race suffers.

Feeling both guilty and powerless, black men and women take turns in the defensive and offensive positions: "Black women ain't no good." Or, "Black men ain't no good." What does this mean for black America? The dominant story that black people "ain't no good" – the myth of black inferiority – is confirmed by us.

When individuals feel badly about themselves, their tendency may be to take flight from the people or situations that spark the bad feelings. Or, they might decide to fight and make the other person feel just as bad. Or, they might struggle for acceptance. Many black women struggle for acceptance, vacillating between trying to make the black man feel strong, competent, and secure and being strong, competent, and secure themselves. The black woman's shame is in not feeling worthy of male attention and care. She therefore gives with one hand while allowing doubt to control with the other.

For black men and women, Cupid's arrow is blocked by the black shadow. When we react to the other as an opponent, it's really gazing at one's own shadow. What I'm saying is that it's your own black shadow you should be concerned with when you're angry and disappointed with your relationship. You have to ask yourself what you're feeling about you, not the other. If you don't feel "womanly" enough, become more dependent, not more independent (it's okay to need others and to ask for help). If you don't feel "manly" enough, become more responsible, not more helpless (nothing beats a failure but a try).

How can we heal from the shame we feel? We have to be courageous. Shameful feelings that we carefully pack away, out of sight from those we love and from ourselves, have to be unpacked in the presence of the other. Only then will the black shadow become conscious, and only then will there be a chance for healing.

The Black Couple's Defense: The White Shadow

We each long for meaning and an experience that connects us to the greater authenticity of life, but it will not come from talking about the problem of the black male or the problem of the black female. The black male and female have the same problem: the belief in black inferiority. Because of it we have sold out to the dominant story of the white man and white woman being more desirable and more able to have successful relationships than we are. We believe whites are better couples and create better families than blacks. Every time we have these thoughts, or fantasize that we're white or with a white partner, we move farther away from being able to develop an authentic self. Authentic self refers to you being who you were created to be. It is you as you are in your body, color, hair, and with your own skills, talents, smarts and character. Development of an authentic self requires you to focus on who you are instead of comparing yourself to whites.

The black man uses the white woman as the measuring stick and the black woman uses the white man as the model mate against which we compare one another in relationships. The great white couple is the story that has unfolded through time and the black couple's hope is to be a white couple.

It makes no sense. Black women view white men as a prize, even though they may be the descendants of the same white men who raped, beat, deprived, and took our children away; who deny, restrict, control and violate our right to life, liberty and the pursuit of happiness; and at the very least who maintain the structures of racism and benefit from our second-class status and our belief in the myth of black inferiority. And black men view white women as the ideal when they were responsible then and even now for their wrongful convictions and harmed lives, and they, too, maintain the structures of racism and benefit from black men's belief in the myth of black inferiority.

Instead of bonding together to fight against the common enemy of racism, we waste our time blaming each other and projecting negative stereotypes and ideas of "nigger" onto the other. But we always end up yearning for an end to the loneliness that comes from alienating the other. When we indulge in these projections and blame, we betray not the other, but ourselves.

Lance and Nancy had been married for 16 years, and they came to see me because they were having problems communicating. It was also revealed that they had not had sex in two months. Lance complained that his wife never took him at his word for anything. She was always asking him the same things over and over. Also, Nancy was always saying she was too tired for sex. For her part, Nancy complained that Lance didn't voluntarily give her all the facts; she had to pull things out of him. Also, Lance didn't help out around the house. He would come home from work, hide behind the newspaper, eat dinner and then later want sex. In the meantime, she'd come home from a long day of work, cook dinner and clean up. Sex was the last thing she was interested in. She was tired.

Lance and Nancy were both executives in corporate America. Lance was the head of his division, a job that carried a lot of responsibility. There was such tension around this couple's communication that I was sure trust was a big issue for each of them, and I hypothesized that the black shadow was keeping them from connecting on a deeper level. The two had met while attending a primarily white University. When asked about their college experiences, Nancy gave me a piece of the puzzle to their relationship dynamic. She'd been one of few females and the only black in her MBA program. She described how she was assigned to do a group project and the other (white) members of her group withheld information from her, which made her look bad and caused her to feel stupid – inferior. It was this experience with her white classmates that made her insecure about having all the facts.

Lance remembered Nancy telling him about it when it happened, but he had never connected that experience to her constant haranguing him for information. When I asked him what that reminded him of, he described his white supervisees constantly questioning his competence and authority, which undermined his self-confidence. Two pieces of the communication puzzle fit into place. Nancy asked Lance to repeat things because she feared not having all the information. Lance perceived Nancy to be questioning his credibility as his white supervisees often did. So they began a dance in which the more Nancy asked him to repeat himself, the more he shut down, and the more he shut down the more suspicious she felt so the more she pushed. Their communication pattern provoked feelings of mutual mistrust, and Nancy's disinterest in sex felt to Lance like another rejection.

It was very helpful for this couple to name the black shadow that was causing them each to feel self-doubt and feelings of inferiority. I suggested that they become allies against the black shadow through their understanding of the other's vulnerability and need for reassurance. Lance and Nancy stopped accusing each other of being withholding and started to talk openly about the discrimination they felt in their lives along with sharing their needs. Lance became more helpful around the house as a result of their new communication and a new feeling of authentic closeness developed. Naturally, they began to have sex again.

The longing that black men and women feel to be mutually cared for and respected is the soul seeking to reclaim the lost "you," and the "I" searching for meaning and connection that will bring it wholeness. Unsure of our human decency and worth, which is fallout from slavery and racism, African American men and women spend too much time pursuing the white shadow, the image of human perfection, and rejecting the loser that is the black shadow – the "nigger" image of the self. The self of the black man/woman that was rejected at birth in America looks for completion in the beloved, but the pursuit ends in failure because the beloved is the same as the rejected self. Unable to retrieve the rejected self, thereby gaining acceptance and a sense of wholeness, the black male-female relationship flounders and we privately and publicly denounce one another for not being white.

The degree to which any of us can be intimate with another is the degree to which we are self-differentiated and have a clear sense of who we are. The black man's/woman's search for an authentic relationship is cut short by his/her confused or negative self-concept. Our romantic relationships inescapably remind us of slavery, the primary wound. Slavery's brush painted black women as ugly and undesirable and black men as irresponsible studs who were also undesirable. Compared to white couples in a culture that believes in white superiority and black inferiority, the black couple is automatically devalued. The black couple does not rank among the white grown-ups. The black stigma locks them out of the "good marriage/healthy family" classification that is reserved for superior white men and women. Marriage thus becomes a fertile ground for the black shadow with the black male/female each projecting feelings of not being beautiful, intelligent, successful, or good enough. Each blames the other for being inadequate, raging against the self and other for being the inferior black that is hated by all – including themselves.

Crossing Over to Interracial Relationships

Some of us cross over to the other side of the street, attempting to out-distance the black shadow through interracial relationships. Others of us go in search of new partners, not understanding that the same problems we've encountered in past relationships will come up again if we haven't confronted the black shadow. Still others avoid relationships, trading relationship gratification for self-concealment in an attempt to suppress the black shadow.

"I am dying on the vine," 47-year-old Marva told me as she talked about being married to a white man. "I want my life back. I'm tired of being on display. I don't feel good about me. I have no identity. I want to feel like a black woman. I'm tired of polite neighbors who would probably not speak to me if it weren't for my white husband. And I am sick to death of his white associates complimenting him on how articulate I am. Am I not supposed to be able to speak the King's English because I'm black? I only feel real when I am among my black people. I would trade living in the suburbs in a huge house for the feeling of realness and true happiness. I can't help but think my life wouldn't be this hard with a black man. No one understands. Even my family sees me as complaining to be complaining."

You can run but you can't hide. Marva was at the age when the black shadow comes in search of you. The isolation and alienation from community and self could no longer be silenced with parenting and moving up the white social ladder. With children approaching college age and having made it up the white social ladder, she had no distractions from the black shadow. Disillusioned and feeling alone, Marva yearned for reconnection with her black roots. Having compromised her authenticity in exchange for the promise of mainstream acceptance, Marva was awakening to the black shadow that had been there all along. Needing space for black self-expression, Marva left her white husband and white picket fence out in the white suburbs and moved back to the city and her own people.

My intent is not to indict any relationship, black or interracial. Simply, I want to illuminate the black shadow that befell us in slavery and that stays with us today through the myth of black inferiority. Love does exist and true intimacy is found in black and interracial relationships, but the black shadow is a trap that too many of us fall into. "Be aware!" is what I'm asking you to do so you too can have the love and relationship you deserve.

Marva's black shadow led her to believe life would be perfect if she could live the white dream. But it was her black shadow that played the part of spoiler. Being a light-skinned black woman she was used to being special in her family and community, but being in a primarily white environment she felt black. Also, her white husband was very demanding and she filtered his many complaints through her internalized belief in black inferiority. He had his own story and his own demons he wrestled with, having grown up poor in South Philadelphia. He, too, was looking for a perfect life, one that made him forget he had ever been poor.

Marva was still running from the black shadow when she left her white husband. She still had work to do, but she was ready to burst after being silent for so many years. She chose to leave rather than to stay and fight for her relationship, but I'm sure the black shadow was right there with her in her next relationship, even with a black man. Changing partners doesn't change the black shadow. Only facing it saps its strength and renders it harmless.

Fear of Commitment

Marriage was once the highly valued turning point in the life cycle of black men and women, a symbol of adulthood, commitment, and moral responsibility. Of course, in slavery this life-preserving and life-affirming ritual was forbidden. Tribal rules and laws about sex and marriage usually connected members to the higher purpose of group solidarity, self-pride and family pride. The slaves who were denied marriage and forced to produce children out of wedlock brought shame on themselves, their families and the group. The unresolved shame and lack of atonement continue to restrict authentic contact between black men and women. In many ways, both men and women still have the impulse to stay apart even when it appears that they actively seek the other.

Commitment and true harmony in the black male-female relationship are affected by the fear of abandonment that each feels in relation to the other. Wrestling with the slave couple's legacy increases their own desire to flee while at the same time causing each person to defend against the flight of the other. Under slavery's spell, the black male and female each longs for the comfort and protection of unity, but each fears commitment. With distrust and fear interfering with their ability to commit to marriage, the black man and woman miss out on a meaningful connection in the cycle of life.

The black male-female relationship was polluted by slavery and myths of white superiority and black inferiority. Consequently, many black men and women today feel unacceptable as mates. Rather than face the mirror reflection of one's self in the other, black men and women seem to deflect unwanted feelings of shame, disappointment, and uncertainty about the responsibilities of married life by staying single. As single men and women, we can avoid the intensity of the black shadow and the daily reminders of being inferior that can be seen in our partners. We can mask the self-hate that has been absorbed for many generations and avoid the critical eye of a discerning partner. We can also escape the close scrutiny of our intimate partners and the expectation of accountability that comes with the commitment of marriage.

While staying single may be a way to deflect some of the painful issues of being black in America, some African American men and women frantically look for somebody – anybody – to assuage the feelings of rejection, loneliness and lack of self-worth. Believing themselves to be damaged goods, these individuals will unconsciously attract partners who behave in ways that recreate in them a sense of worthlessness, bringing them closer to the black shadow, which they were trying to keep at a distance. For many black women, being single is akin to having a disease. It deepens the sense of not being the one chosen, of being devalued and maligned by both white and black society. Thus, it is particularly hurtful to watch the rising number of black men marrying white women as we sit off to the sideline experiencing the shame of being black and single.

The real essence of marriage is in the partners' ability to make a commitment to the other. Who you are and what you represent determines the credibility of your commitment. When possessed by the black shadow, the black man/woman is not acquainted with the real self and therefore is not a credible partner. Vulnerable to the currents of slavery and the winds of racism that cause self-doubt, group rejection, and acceptance of white superiority, just how good is your word in a relationship? Ask the black shadow.

Striking Out: Domestic Violence

Lacking inner peace and harmony, some black men strike out violently at the black women in their lives. There are many ways to look at this tragic act: the man is frustrated and takes it out on the only person below him on the totem pole of racism: his woman. The man is a "nigger" so what else should we expect of him but dangerous, animal behavior? The man is justified because black women are emasculating. I view black male batterers as men who are deep in the embrace of their black shadows.

So far away from the spirit of kinship and cooperation that Mother Africa taught its children, the black shadow erupts violently in the black men who emotionally, physically and sexually abuse their female partners. The bullied, downtrodden black man becomes the all-powerful bully. The need for control of self takes him out of control with her. He becomes his black shadow, acting out his self-hate and rage on her. She is the reflection of his lost dreams of confident manhood, power and hopefulness. He is the boy locked out of his own manhood, pounding on the door of his own soul. He yearns for strength and flashes his fists with a surge of adrenaline, but when the storm inside him subsides, he finds only pathetic weakness. Then he becomes the boy, pleading with his mother/wife/sister/daughter for forgiveness and selfishly asking for pity instead of pledging himself to self-awareness so it won't happen again.

He must accept psychological responsibility for understanding and healing the black shadow within that he so violently projects out. The black woman must not endure more violence, rape and brutality at the hands of the black man because she has confused self-sacrifice with undeserved loyalty.

There are scores of black women enduring intimate partner violence (IPV) at the hands of black men. Many African Americans see IPV as part of the scenery in crime-infested, poor black communities. But IPV crosses class and education barriers. It happens to professional black women living in the well-off suburbs as well as unemployed black women living in the projects. Traditionally, black women have remained silent about these assaults on their bodies and minds in order to protect black men from the racist legal system. They sacrifice their own well-being for the safety of their abusers. But women's bodies and minds must not become dumpsters for black men's anger, rage and need to feel powerful in a racist world. IPV is as wrong as racism. Black men who batter women must be held accountable. I have faith that people can change, and I pray that abusers learn to control themselves and make amends for their behavior. Unfortunately, change doesn't happen that easily, so we need to make sure abusers really have reformed before we allow them back into a situation where they might hurt another woman.

Discovering their intrinsic beauty and self-worth is the best way black women can avoid becoming victims of IPV. They understand that they deserve to be treated with respect and consideration and they won't be silent about IPV or any of its warning signs. All of us in the black community must confront this issue with openness and compassion so that our loved ones can get help. It is absolutely crucial in order to restore the balance, harmony, dignity, respect and unity that will create a protected environment against racism in the black home and community.

Self-Knowledge is Vital to Healthy Black Relationships

Every one of us must become aware of our skills and talents and what drives us to reach or not reach full realization of our skills and talents. It's this self-knowledge that creates healthy relationships because the self gives us meaning, direction and purpose. It helps us to understand our own needs and the interlocking needs of others – the "I" and "You" of soul that makes each one of us complete. Healing our relationships means engaging in genuine conversation, but that requires each partner to show up with self-knowledge. We have to trade our projections – the stories we tell ourselves about others – for vulnerability. We have to give up mistrust of the other for self-honesty. We have to let go of separation and choose connection. We have to substitute complexity for multiplicity, and get rid of fear and choose intimacy.

My black shadow is very sensitive to trust. I heard repeatedly growing up that black men are not trustworthy. One day, I became upset because my partner had not shared information with me that I thought he should have. In an email (I chose to communicate in writing so I could balance my emotions and intellect), I wrote, "I am trying to understand our differences in style and not to make more of it than it is. Thus, I am writing to express my disappointment in your level of communication regardless of significance. I do understand that you do not intend me harm when you simply don't think a thing is important or worthy of sharing. However, I need you to understand that by not sharing things with me it affects my sense of trust." This communication was my way of facing my black shadow, which was telling me that my partner was just another black man not to be trusted and that I was just another black woman unworthy of being valued.

My partner responded, "I am sorry that I caused you hurt by not going into every little detail. I thought I was doing the right thing when I communicated with you. It appears that I am damned if I do and damned if I don't. The one thing I do know and that is I love you and we will work it out. I'm not perfect, but I will continue to strive to be better."

His black shadow could have been thinking, "A black man just can't please a black woman so why bother?" But he didn't fall into that trap. He and I expressed our feelings without pointing fingers and blaming each other for being inherently flawed as black mates, even though the black shadow was hanging around waiting for us to give in to the myth of black inferiority. My beloved lifted my spirits with these words: "Problems are temporary if we can stand and not lay down to them. We will get through them together."

We each bear the legacy of slavery trauma, but we also have a history we can claim from before slavery. Learning about African culture and relationship rituals is a way of filling in the blanks left by slavery and giving us a sense of ourselves beyond racism's "nigger" definition. And most of all, it's a sanctuary for our spirit to have a vision of love of self and love of other that existed for our black people before we were mastered with a false sense of self through the myth of black inferiority.

Unchained Together
And unto him she said, I see your chained heart.
Crying out to me, asking my forgiveness.
Would you could save me,
Your queen.
I would not have borne babes out of Africa.
And unto her he said, I hear your fear.
No words need you speak.
In sorrow I turn toward birth.
Awakened by your grace and courage.
Was once king will be—
Home again.
—MFW

Exercises for Black Couples

Once a week, set aside time to do these exercises together. Find a quiet place, turn off the phones and spend a few minutes breathing and relaxing together before you get started.

Step 1: Begin by sharing your thoughts and feelings about this chapter. What did you read that helped you have a deeper understanding of yourself and your relationship? What made you uncomfortable? What did you recognize about yourself and your beloved? Do you notice any bad habits you fall into as the black man/woman in the relationship that might trace back to slave history? Discuss what you might want to do differently?

Step 2: Do a shared visualization to get in touch with the underlying trauma of the legacy of slavery so you can begin to heal. Start by holding hands and looking into each other's eyes. Now imagine you are slaves together and imagine the pain you feel on witnessing your beloved's agony and suffering. Your partner is imagining the same about you. What does he/she need? What is she/he missing? Talk about what you imagine this experience would have been like – to love someone who was enslaved and to be enslaved yourself. Bring these truths into your heart and let them sit there for a moment. Say aloud, "This is what happened to our ancestors just a few generations ago." Give thanks that slavery is ended and forgive each other for all the ways you let each other down. Resolve to become more conscious and more mindful in the future. To end the exercise, thank your beloved for engaging in this healing process with you.

Step 3: Practice daily gratitude and appreciation of your beloved and your relationship. Every day or every week, write down the things you appreciate and place them in a jar. On your anniversary, sit down together and read through all the notes of appreciation.

Chapter 7
Divided Over Class

The myth of black inferiority upholds a rigid black class system. Like in any group, money and success are sought after, and those who have it enjoy prestige among their peers. But in the black community the meaning of success is tied to our belief in the lie of black inferiority. Not having money and not succeeding make us feel that we're "nigger." Spouses, family members and friends may secretly be glad when we fail because our success only amplifies their feelings of black inferiority. We may worry so much about success that it stops us from taking professional risks because failure is more dangerous to those who labor under the lie that they are inferior because of the color of their skin.

The unemployed and poor blame themselves for being inferior rather than understanding their failure in the context of systematic racism, which puts tremendous obstacles in the paths of black people. Limited educational and economic opportunities undermine our ability to get ahead. But for many black people, it is still hard to separate racism from lack of personal competence. In our heart of hearts we wonder if we're the problem. Do we lack fundamental talents and skills? Are we just not good enough because we're black?

The question of whether blacks are competent enough should not even be asked! We are individual human beings with a wide diversity of skills, talents and gifts, yet we are still measured and judged as a group, and we still measure and judge ourselves this way! That is the black shadow at work in our unconscious minds, that keeps us believing that the lie of black inferiority is really true.

Just as much as we fear failure, many of us are also highly conflicted about success. When we make it – get our degrees, land a good job, earn a good living, own nice things, give our children nice things and rich opportunities – we often feel disloyal to those left behind in our families and neighborhoods. We feel guilty for doing well, and worry that we'll be alienated from our community, called "oreo" (a white-acting black), "sell-out" or worse. At times, we take on the role of family savior out of misplaced guilt. Or we break ties with our embarrassing black families and move out to the white suburbs so we won't be associated with those people (or, more accurately, those "niggers").

I see this latter group in my therapy office. These clients come in feeling sad and tired, not realizing that their weariness and unhappiness is connected to their self-exile from their community. I help them to understand that they are rejecting their roots and the support of the people who love them. They are losing the chance to reach back and help others as role models and mentors. They are losing opportunities to learn from elders and friends who may not be financially successful, but who have other wisdom to share.

Cross-Projections: A Pattern of Blame

When we project a movie onto a screen, we can't see the screen as it actually is; we can only see the images playing on it. In the same way, we project our undesirable thoughts, feelings, desires, motivations and more onto other people and then we can't really see them – we're only able to see our own image projected onto them. This is a problem every human being faces, because projection is a psychological defense mechanism that all of us use at some time or another. When it comes to class issues in the black community, we frequently project our fear that we're not good enough onto less-successful or more-successful blacks. I call it "cross-class projections." This is important to understand because it's an unconscious process that is harmful to ourselves and to others. Busy projecting our negative ideas onto others and blaming them for our unhappiness, we fail to see how these projections make our lives and the lives of our fellow African Americans much harder. We divide instead of uniting to battle the real problem in all of our lives: the black shadow.

Cross-projections are our mind's attempt to relieve anxiety and tension in the self. The problem is, they make it impossible for us to have real relationships because we're so busy throwing our negative ideas onto the other person. I worked with a successful black business executive named Camille who had it all: a loving husband, three children who were thriving in their private school, and the love and respect of her family. Well – almost all of her family. Her only brother, Johnny, resented Camille's success. Chronically unemployed, he had always been the problem child in the family. Each Thanksgiving and Christmas he was a no-show for the "dinners at the Big House," as he called the family gatherings his sister hosted in her manicured, upper-middle-class neighborhood. Johnny referred to her family holiday celebrations as "the master calling the slaves in from the field on a special occasion." Whenever they were together he rejected his sister's overtures of friendship and accused her of being an "oreo." Over time, he refused to attend any family event that included Camille.

The black shadow says things like, "Black people don't want you to get ahead. They will hold you back any way they can. And don't let them think they've made it because then they think they're better than you. Give them a little position and they act like they own the place." Feeling bad to begin with from internalized black inferiority, we relate to other blacks with envy, jealousy and competitiveness when they achieve financial and professional success. We psychologically compensate for our own sense of inferiority by accusing the other of feeling superior. Used to being in a one-down position to whites, we can resent successful blacks because they are a mirror of our failure. So we project our fears and judgments onto them and accuse them of being "uppity." We expect successful blacks to act white because we African Americans have internalized the belief that blacks are intellectually inferior. The circular logic tells us that a black person who achieves success must be more white than black. That's how Johnny felt about his sister. When we're around educated, professional, wealthy blacks and we end up resenting them, it's because our black shadows make us feel inferior – not because those people are causing us to feel inferior.

Camille and Johnny were caught in a power struggle around her success and his battle with his black shadow. Johnny's way of dealing with his feelings of inferiority was to go on the attack. Holding the inferior position and wanting to feel powerful, he looked for ways to belittle and humiliate Camille. The black shadow made him mean. He rationalized his behavior by blaming her, but he never blamed the true culprit: the myth of black inferiority that made him feel like success was impossible for him because he was defective by definition as a black man.

Camille felt like she couldn't win with Johnny. No matter what she did, he viewed it as patronizing, or accused her of rubbing her success in his face. "I miss my brother," she told me. "I don't feel like he ever sees me. Not since I went off to college and he dropped out of high school. Now that Mom and Dad are gone, we're the only family we have, and he won't even come for Christmas. He hates me and I never did anything to him. I can't win with him."

Camille and her brother had not reconciled when she left therapy. It was a loss that she felt deeply, but she had to accept that she couldn't heal the relationship without Johnny's cooperation. She resolved to be forgiving and open to reconciliation when Johnny was ready. She continues to send invitations that go unanswered.

The Talented Tenth

There may be some truth to the accusations that those blacks who make it in the white world feel superior to other African Americans. The talented tenth can be self-righteous and judgmental of less successful blacks, echoing some of the same criticisms as white America. "Blacks are always blaming racism or the white man for their failure. When are they going to take responsibility for their lack of ambition and work ethic?" When we say that blacks are not victimized by racism and it's their own inherent inadequacy that results in their massive failure, we are really saying that the problem is racial inferiority. Below their veneer of self-confidence and smugness lies the black shadow. The talented tenth project their own self-rejection onto their lower class brothers and sisters, accusing them of being shiftless, lazy, lacking ambition and not taking personal responsibility for their lives. If they stopped projecting, they would see their brothers and sisters struggling to be valued and find self-worth in a world that judges and curses them for being black. In other words, if we would only stop projecting our fears onto one another, empathy, understanding and compassion would blossom and we could become allies instead of enemies. Ultimately, we all pay the price for believing that the real struggle in black America is between the classes and not with racism.

The ability to move up from poverty to the middle class creates an illusion that blacks can be fully accepted into the dominant white system, igniting fear and anxiety in the entire group. The black middle class is fearful of lower-class behavior that might interfere with their complete integration into the white mainstream; and the black lower class is fearful of being rejected by both white and middle-class black America, affirming their inferior status. These fears manifest as obsessive worrying and complaining about the behavior of the other. The black projection process keeps us hopelessly entangled while white supremacy is ignored. It's the black shadow at work. It keeps us divided, and it keeps us blaming one another rather than pointing the finger at the true culprit.

Understanding Class as a Symbol of Racism

For African Americans, making it into the middle class is about finally being accepted into human (white) society. The white middle class is the norm against which everyone else is compared and measured. As black Americans, we need to understand class as a symbol of racism. What does class represent at the unconscious level? Like the saying, "Clothes make the man," becoming middle class implies that the worth of a black person is considered (not guaranteed) only after she or he achieves financial success. The full humanity of whites is never questioned, but for blacks it's always unconsciously questioned so class status has different ramifications in black America. For example, whites view class mobility as an incentive for working harder and gaining more privilege in a society that already automatically confers privilege on them for their white skin. For blacks, it's a different story. Class mobility is a way of disproving the myth of black inferiority, a way of gaining some power and privilege, although always limited because of the second-class status of the dark-skinned.

What is the real function of class within an already devalued group? We have seen how society looks at class and classifies minorities. Jews and Asians are viewed as middle and upper-middle class (although there are many who are struggling and working class) and they are regarded by the white-dominated society as smart, ambitious and successful. Blacks are seen as poor and working class and we are regarded as lazy, not as smart, inherently inferior – all the "nigger" stereotypes. The myth of black inferiority that conceals racism and oppression leads to black shame for African Americans.

Class Dues

Scorned by society for being black, and rejected by one's own family for either making it or not making it up the social ladder, we fall prey to self-isolation, group alienation and feelings of hopelessness. Hurt and lonely, some of us attempt to bypass our feelings by disassociating ourselves from our brothers and sisters. Others of us try to avoid feelings of guilt by putting other blacks down. Still others try to win approval and acceptance by giving and giving.

"I'm always the one to fix everything for everybody," 34-year-old Phyllis told me one day in therapy. "My mother calls me, my sister calls me, my brother calls me. But who do I call? No one is ever there for me. Nobody even asks how I'm doing. When I feel lonely and depressed, there's no one for me to call. I'm supposed to just get over things. Be strong. Suck it up."

Phyllis was a successful entrepreneur and ran her own business. Although still a young woman, she was already the most affluent person in her family. Because of her new class status, her family assigned her the role of family savior. In many black families, one member's success is the success of the whole family; especially since it typically requires the pooled efforts and resources of family members to launch one successful individual. How well the successful child – the savior – maintains the implicit oath of loyalty to the family is judged by his or her ability to shoulder the never-ending emotional and financial debt without complaint. That's what happened to Phyllis. Her siblings constantly asked for loans that they never repaid. They asked her to co-sign on a lease for her brother who had a terrible credit rating and was deeply in debt. Already stressed with running her business, Phyllis felt like there was no support for her. She felt her family members were taking advantage of her, but she was too self-conscious of her new status and privilege to stand up for herself and set healthy boundaries. As we worked together in therapy, Phyllis also examined her guilt at being the lightest skinned child in her family, and her anger and despair at how her mother had expected more of her but less of her darker-skinned siblings.

The savior, despite educational and financial success, is in danger of living an unlived life because of the guilt which forces him/her to do for family members without personal regard for self. Other family members are also at risk for limited self-development because learned helplessness is the likely result of relying on one person to meet the success needs of an entire family. It teaches some individuals not to live up to their full potential but to function as racial inferiors.

The old adaptive strategy of dealing with racism by ensuring one member's success is neither useful nor effective today. It doesn't create a supportive family environment where all members can achieve their highest potential. And it doesn't lend itself to the superior functioning of African Americans as a group because self-sufficiency, intelligence and resiliency should be encouraged in every family member, not just one or two chosen ones. Moreover, it provokes shame, envy, anxiety, guilt and group fragmentation as a result of the class conflict in families and in the black community. Caught up in class issues, we're continually diverted from the real problem of white supremacy. Divided, blindly acting and reacting, projecting and blaming, we bind our hands in the fight against racism. As quarterback, the unacknowledged black shadow inhibits consistent motion toward real problem identification and solution, short-circuiting our ability to develop our maximum potential. Our failure to perceive the real problem of white supremacy and to keep our attention centered on it leaves us chasing our tails.

Passing on Class Confusion

Adults are role models for children, and parents transmit their attitudes and feelings about class to their children a thousand times a day. Parents' buried conflicts, denied dreams, hidden worries and unspoken fears about success and failure are part of the air the family breathes. Children absorb it consciously and unconsciously, and in this way they learn negative attitudes that put their self-development at risk. Just before I graduated from college, my grandmother put her fears about class in writing. "Dear Faye," she wrote, "Just because you're graduating from college doesn't mean that you're better than your mother."

I was shocked that my beloved grandmother would ever believe that I would think of myself as better than anyone else because of my education. None of her children had gone to college, and I was the first of her grandchildren to graduate. It took me some time to understand where this letter was coming from. My grandmother suffered a lifetime of pain from family members ignoring her, neglecting her and leaving her behind because she was dark and poor. I absorbed the guilt of that letter and consequently moved back to the same city as my family even though my dream had been to move across the country to California. After reading that letter, there was no way I would betray my family by moving away. No one could accuse me of thinking I was better than anyone else.

Unfortunately for some, spoken and unspoken family messages about whether it's possible to get out of poverty and/or worries about members leaving others behind prevent some from even trying. When I provided couple and family therapy services to substance dependent inmates behind the walls of a prison in the Philadelphia area, there were sometimes three generations of a family in prison and I personally know four generations of a family living in a subsidized housing development (project). This alone tells me we are passing on assumptions to our children and grandchildren about black inferiority and class. The class shadow in black America is certain to appear in the lives of our children and their children's lives like all the other shadowy issues if we don't develop a real understanding of the myth of black inferiority.

Gregory, a 15-year-old tenth grader, was referred to treatment for academic failure and educational apathy by the school psychologist. Psychological testing revealed normal intelligence and no major emotional disturbance. As an only child, Gregory was very attuned to his parents' feelings even though the family spoke little of their feelings. His father worked in the private sector and secretly felt that he had to check his blackness at the door when he got to work. Dad felt lonely and isolated, rarely seeing old friends and family except for obligatory holiday visits. Mom was also unhappy in her office surrounded by whites waiting to pounce on any mistake that might prove that affirmative action really was the only reason for her being in a high-level executive position. Both she and her husband had grown up poor and both had internalized feelings of shame at having been black and poor.

Gregory sensed that his parents felt trapped by their success and their repressed feelings about racism. Sensitive to black inferiority, his parents pushed and prodded him to succeed, admonishing him not to become another black statistic and reminding him of the horror of being black and poor. But individually, they each felt unworthy, devalued and trapped. Without any way to talk about the mixed messages he was getting from his parents – "Succeed and be as unhappy as we are!" – Gregory chose to underachieve.

As he failed his classes, Gregory adopted an arrogant attitude about school. He told me he was intellectually superior to his classmates, but the work was too beneath him, which is why he didn't bother studying. False pride masked his fear of black inferiority. Well-defended and guarded against his painful feelings, Gregory spent most of his time with white friends in his suburban neighborhood pretending that racism had nothing to do with him.

The turning point for this family came when his parents finally opened up about their struggles as upper-middle-class black success stories. Gregory, who often looked at his phone and texted his friends during therapy, gave his parents his full attention and soaked up every word they said. It was the truth he'd needed them to speak aloud. He was able to voice his own uncertainties about succeeding as a black man, and his parents realized that they had to be more honest with themselves and one another about the toll it was taking on them, and also about the lessons they'd learned that might help their son navigate these new waters for middle-class black Americans.

Racism, along with black America's preoccupation with class differences, threatens to keep our children from staying in the middle-class or rising higher. Unconscious of the black shadow in our lives, we reinforce destructive patterns and model for our children incomplete lives and shame-based identities.

Class Shame

Poverty shames African Americans. We hear white sociologists talk about the "transgenerational nature of poverty" and "culture of poverty" and we feel ashamed that we're somehow doomed to live impoverished lives. We also believe the lie that we're constitutionally unable to rise, and so it becomes a self-fulfilling prophecy. Possessed by the black shadow, we African Americans internalize society's negative predictions for us. Psychologically cut off from our authentic selves because of the lie of black inferiority, we don't challenge their statistics and predictions; we accept them as true and blame ourselves, or project our shame and blame onto our brothers and sisters.

Shame is intensely personal, but we also share it as a community. Superficially, it keeps us involved with one another and at the same time that it leads to class stratification. Shame encourages cross-class projections, leaving us all hungry for acceptance and approval. Shame discourages us from consciously acknowledging the black shadow at the root of black class dynamics. Shame divides family members when one succeeds and the others don't and makes us all disrespectful. Like fighting in a loveless marriage, shame is the passion that keeps the class war alive in black America.

Chris, a 30-year-old married man with two children, came to therapy to talk about problems with his job. A laborer with a high school diploma, he dreamed of having an office job where he could wear Armani suits and Ferragamo shoes. *GQ* magazine was his bible, and he resented his college-educated wife for not sharing his lifestyle aspirations. She was not into designer clothes and dressing to impress.

Both Chris and his wife had grown up in the projects. While Chris's family had moved up from the projects, his wife's family remained there. Chris had been attracted to his wife's intelligence and was disappointed that she didn't get a master's degree. Chris berated her for not wanting more and badmouthed her family for still living in the projects.

Chris was blaming her as a way to mask his own shame at being less educated and less financially successful than his wife. He projected those feelings onto his wife, and it caused problems in their marriage. He was intellectually insecure with low self-confidence, so when they first married he believed his wife's success would be his success. Through her, he would achieve his desired middle-class image. Disappointed with each other and the marriage, he and his wife battled viciously. He belittled her values and made degrading remarks about her appearance. She mocked him for being uneducated, which was a sore spot for Chris. In school and at home, he had internalized negative expectations about his intellectual capabilities until he was afraid to even try to be a good student. Chris's family members lived within blocks of one another and were overly involved in one another's life. To the outside they appeared to be a very loving family who watched each other's back. However, they were really watching each other's back to see if anyone got ahead of someone else.

There was an unspoken family rule that said: "We must all stay the same." As a result, they put one another down and constantly compared themselves and their children to the others. Who had the prettiest child? Who had the best house? Who was driving the nicest car? Who was the smartest? Who made the most money? For them, it was a vicious circle of trying to outdo the other – escape the black shadow and that feeling of not being good enough.

Shame can create family envy. Family envy can diminish individual spirit and block self-authenticity. It can dampen or take away a person's will to succeed. When an individual's own dreams and ambitions are not realized, she or he may feel envious of others. Feeling jealous of the person who has succeeded, we project our envy onto our brothers and sisters, blaming them for making us feel inferior. On the flip side, when an individual succeeds, she or he may feel guilty. Feeling guilty for leaving others behind, we project our guilt onto our brothers and sisters, resenting them for reminding us that we were once in that inferior place.

There are two sides to every coin. On one side, shame holds us back. On the other side, shame motivates us to do better. Shame about growing up in poverty motivated 42-year-old Shirley to work her way through college and graduate school. She wanted a better life for herself and her children. Working hard in

CHAPTER 7 – DIVIDED OVER CLASS

corporate America, she was passed over for promotions again and again, those higher-paying jobs automatically going to young white males. Shirley felt angry, but she also felt deep shame at being a black woman, but it was unconscious – her black shadow. Determined to prove that her blackness was not an issue, she worked harder and remained silent about racism. At work she accepted the role of "good black." At home, all hell broke loose. She screamed, cursed and physically fought with her husband and daughter. All her rage and shame was taken out on them.

Anxious and ashamed of personal feelings of incompetence, she obsessively focused on her daughter's school performance. Fearful that her daughter, Maya, would fail (her own misplaced fear) she imposed strict rules including no dating. Maya was 17, and objected strenuously – all her friends had been dating for years. But Shirley wouldn't hear it. She accused her daughter of being a whore. In her mind, she was imagining the pregnancy that would ruin her daughter's life. What she couldn't see was how her black shame was not letting her see that her daughter was a responsible, mature young woman with her own ambitions and dreams. Like many adolescents, Maya rebelled by doing what her mother feared: she failed her exams.

A combination of family therapy and individual sessions with the mother and daughter helped them to lower their defenses, stop pointing the finger at the other and start to talk about their hidden fears. From watching her mother's struggles, Maya had come to believe that black success in corporate America was a blueprint for unhappiness. Her mother had spent so much time at work she'd barely been around for Maya when she was young. Maya felt happiest at her aunt's house – the "unsuccessful" aunt who seemed happy in comparison to Shirley.

Shirley admitted that she had been unhappy, but not because of her job. She actually loved her work and found great satisfaction in solving problems and being seen as an expert in her field. She explained to herself and Maya that what made her unhappy was not knowing how to speak up for herself when she felt unfairly treated by her manager, and feeling like the work environment was fundamentally unsafe and unwelcoming for a black woman. Making a distinction between her frustration at racism and her satisfaction with her intellectual life helped Maya reclaim her ambition to be a lawyer, which eventually she realized. I worked with Shirley to find ways to face her own fears and empower herself to deal with racism in the workplace. She stopped worrying about others' perception of her as an angry black woman and she filed a discrimination suit against her employer.

The Black Caste System

Sensitive to rejection and devaluation, black people created a black caste system way back during the days of slavery. It determined who was superior and who was inferior within our own ranks. The light-skinned house slaves were superior to the dark-skinned slaves who did the back-breaking labor in the fields. The black caste system was first determined by skin color and hair, and when we had access to it education became the third factor and financial success the fourth. Lighter skin and good hair, education and financial success were equated with a less black-referenced ("nigger") self and increased chance of acceptance by whites.

There are so many problems with the black caste system, and first and foremost is using white acceptance as the highest aspiration for a black person. That is the black shadow's agenda. Creating caste/class divisions within our families and communities only makes life harder for us. We are doing this to ourselves, but it's our black shadows calling the tune. It controls us with the dual swords of shame and humiliation. The black caste system divides us and keeps us from putting our energy into dismantling racism.

The black shadow provokes in us feelings of inferiority and the desire for white approval, and our enslavement to those lies divides us from other blacks. We hide our deepest longing and ambitions from one another to protect our dreams from scorn, mockery, negativity and incredulity. We hide our fear of failure by rationalizing that the odds are against us and then attack those who do succeed because their triumphs make us feel like losers. We succeed in spite of the odds, and feel like imposters at home, where we're not allowed to voice our insecurities. We distrust blacks from other classes and doubt one another's motives and sincerity. We can't think the best of one another because we can't think the best of ourselves. The black shadow feeds on our insecurity, humiliation and shame.

Imagine if one person in a family challenged the myth of black inferiority. Imagine the ripple effect on the entire family system. How else will we ever replace self-hate with self-love?

A black family with soul can talk honestly and openly about how the legacy of slavery impacts their lives in very personal ways. They can talk about how the myth of black inferiority undermines their confidence and ability to value themselves fully as human beings, and they can support and empathize with one another. I have also seen black families hold members accountable for ending internal family racism by challenging the little comments, the snide remarks, the sniff of disapproval, the toxic silence, the cut-offs and gossip.

Bringing our own black shadow attitudes out into the open is the only way to take the power back. Black families with soul know how to love, and we know how to be there for one another, and best of all we can deeply trust one another to embrace diversity and genuine connection over artificial values of skin color, hair, class and imposed sameness. They model for all of us how to make home a place of allies you can count on in the fight against external racism, and also internal racism.

Great Expectations

African Americans hope and believe that financial success and joining the middle class will transform feelings of worthlessness into positive self-esteem. But the lie of black inferiority was invented alongside the lie of white superiority, so being black and in the middle-class doesn't change one's position in society. It's the dark skin, not the bank account or address that is the problem and it can't be changed. But it explains why some African Americans feel depressed despite their upwardly mobile life paths. They still suffer from feelings of emptiness, loneliness, powerlessness and hopelessness because they still have their black shadow. It doesn't go away when they move to the 'burbs. They are even loneliner than before because no one understands their pain because the rest of our community regards them as having made it and turned their backs.

Insecure people spend a lot of time and money trying to impress others. The same goes for middle-class blacks. Needing approval and acceptance, some live from paycheck to paycheck, spending our money on what we hope will pass for class in the form of DKNY, Versace, Calvin Klein, and the like. Driving our BMW, Lexus or Mercedes, we attempt to alleviate the feeling of inferiority. Teaching our children to look for pride in a pair of designer jeans, we forget to teach them basic black self-respect and self-love. These outward symbols of success and status have no lasting or real effect on the black shadow, and they only bring us temporary relief from our anxiety and insecurity that we're not good enough no matter how good we are. And once again, we turn our own insecurity around and project our negative feelings and fears onto other blacks. We look down on those who have less than we have, and we also look down on those who have more than we have.

The bottom line is that our anxious need to prove we're different from the group epitomizes our collective fear of being judged a "nigger." Using superficial degrees of separation such as physical appearance, education, income, speech and where we live, we attempt to manage feelings of black inferiority. More importantly, we falsely believe that we can correct the myth of black inferiority through artificial degrees of separation.

We can't. It's not working! With the myth of black inferiority firmly in place, we experience psychological numbness, social rejection and cultural confusion at home. Collective black survival is therefore compounded by each individual's sensitivity to and fear of the black shadow. Sensing that at the core of each black person is a "nigger" in waiting, we are always off balance. We act out the racism that we abhor by making statements like, "I don't want to live next door to blacks," and "I don't want a black lawyer/doctor/plumber." The place to start healing from our own internalized racism is to honestly examine the legacy of slavery trauma we inherited, and once and for all heal from it so we and our children and our children's children can be free of it.

Knowledge is a healer. Knowledge is a gift for developing your real self. Where there is bitterness, knowledge is absent, and where knowledge is, there is also forgiveness. The path to health and healing for African Americans is paved with black shadow awareness. Knowledge of the black shadow is the missing wisdom in our class battles.

It's the black shadow that makes us feel bad. Standing in judgment of one another, criticizing and comparing and competing with one another, we aren't taking responsibility for the black shadow. We are victims turned jailers without black shadow awareness. African Americans have always believed that out of no way, a way would come. Our belief in God kept hope alive in the black community during slavery and the Jim Crow days. As individuals, families and a community, we must believe in our collective strength and use it to do this crucial work.

Exercises
Confronting the Class Shadow

Here are 5 steps to confronting the class shadow. Try them on your own and with your loved ones; then talk about them at school, in your church, at family reunions. It's time to get the conversation started and drive away the black shadow.

Step 1: Think about what makes it hard for you to relate to the other classes (for example, feelings of inadequacy, inferiority or superiority.) Write down any insights you have about black shame, and about family and group pressures that create self-doubt and/or guilt related to class.

Step 2: Make a list of all the personal advantages and disadvantages you've experienced from the class system. (For example, education, beauty, money, security, safety.)

Step 3: Challenge the myths of black inferiority and the myths of white superiority in every situation where it comes up, including with family, co-workers and friends. Work on balancing your emotions with critical thinking so you can find strategic ways to educate yourself and others.

Step 5: Appreciate your individual uniqueness while respecting the group. Explore ways that you can both be part of your black community while at the same time not feeling responsible for what other black people do. This is a subtle process, so it might help to write down the insights you have and chart your progress.

Chapter 8
Dismantling the Collective Black Box

"One day I walked into the cafeteria where most of the staff eat lunch," Jacqui, a 32-year-old hospital internist told me. "I sat down at the table where the medical technicians were eating and the conversation stopped. I couldn't understand what had happened. I tried to join in, but everyone just stared at me. We were all about the same age, but they saw me as a physician, and somewhere down the line it was decided that staff and physicians shouldn't mix. I was effectively kept out even though I wanted to be a part of their group. It's really tough. They see me differently. Now I feel uncomfortable. I can't be myself."

When Jacqui first talked about feelings of isolation on the job, I assumed that she was talking about exclusion by white coworkers. I was wrong. It was a group of black medical technicians who made her feel unwelcome. Having heard her whole life from black schoolmates, "You talk like a white girl," Jacqui had already learned to be self-conscious around her own people. This experience reminded her of many other times she had been excluded by other blacks.

"What's wrong with me?" she asked me. "Why don't I know how to relate to them? What could I be doing differently? Why can't I make them feel comfortable with me?"

The collective black box is another way of talking about cliques. There isn't just one collective black box; there are lots of them, and each one struggles for acceptance and the right to belong. The black middle class, the black lower class, light-skin, dark-skin, bad-ass niggers, etc. are all examples of collective black boxes. These are closed groups of individuals connected by a characteristic, trait or interest. Membership to this group requires sameness; differences are grounds for exclusion. Black cliques create a sense of safety and belonging for its members, but there is a cost: if you deviate from the group norm, you're out. It's the collective black box that made my nephew, Gary, drop out of high school so he could prove he was a hoodlum like his friends, and it was the collective black box that excluded him in prison when he decided to go back to school and turn his life around.

African Americans' fixation with "our kind" may go all the way back to our tribal heritage. Perhaps we exclude our own brothers and sisters as a way to make ourselves feel powerful, or because we feel envy or fear. Whatever the reason, excluding others who are different in some fundamental way – class, relationship status, sexual orientation, gender orientation, skin tone – causes more pain and suffering to black people. It divides our already besieged community into us/them. Someone like Jacqui, who is excluded from this close sharing with the black professionals in her workplace, has a tough time trying to fit in. Those black medical technicians saw she was a doctor and classified her as "them," not "us." They closed ranks and shut her out without ever giving her a chance. She was only allowed to have a single identity – doctor – and was not allowed also to be a thirty-something sister looking for friendship from other blacks.

The Collective Identity

The myth of black inferiority leaves us believing that blacks are a monolithic group. The reality is that we are each unique, but we have a hard time allowing one another to be all that we can be. Diversity in our own community makes us feel threatened. For example, it has taken us a long time as a community to accept our homosexual and bisexual brothers and sisters and own up to our own discomfort with diverse sexualities. The black shadow within us makes us stifle other people's dreams and aspirations by insisting they conform to the group's standards.

"Black people don't do that," is what an African American girl was told when she wanted a guitar so she could become a folk musician.

"What's wrong with you?" a black boy is challenged when he admits to preferring classical music to rap. The collective black box clamps down on our individuality, interfering with our development of an authentic self.

We can trace this back to slavery, when our humanity was denied by white slavers and we were punished for expressing our individuality – our emotions, hopes, dreams, talents, gifts, joys. We learned to be "nigger" to survive, but we are each unique individuals. The collective black box is a leftover problem from slavery. Settling for the collective identity, individual African Americans are unseen, unacknowledged and disregarded in both white and black America.

Individuality is essential to emotional well-being, but we have to struggle to hear the call of the self over the black collective.

African Americans are made to board the "either-or" train. The black family and community make it hard for individuals to claim their individuality and retain their group identity at the same time. Individuals are frequently scapegoated when they dare to be different from their families or the group. We accuse them of being disloyal to the family or the race. We regard them as traitors.

The black clique at Jacqui's hospital may not have consciously thought they were punishing Jacqui, but that's what it felt like to her when they excluded her. Why do we punish someone who did well? Do we believe others' success means there is less success available for the rest of us? We need to examine our knee-jerk rejections of our own brothers and sisters who succeed, who fail and whose paths take them down roads that are unfamiliar to the black collective. We need to support individuality, but to do that we have to ask ourselves what makes us uncomfortable about diversity? What makes us angry? Would we have wanted Jacqui to give up her dreams and plans to be a doctor and settle for being a medical technician, which was not her dream, just so she could feel a sense of belonging?

The black collective identity is damaging to both the individual and the group. It functions to derail or destroy our individuality. It results in self and group estrangement, and that only strengthens the myth of black inferiority while disabling us.

Collective Denial

One of the most evil aspects of racism is that it teaches us to blame ourselves for the misfortunes of being black. Internalized blame becomes learned self-hate, and that turns into the collective black box, which perpetuates actions, feelings and behaviors that keep us working against ourselves. We blame the victim (ourselves) and then victimize the victim (one a other).

When I think about our collective denial that slavery is the primary wound of our people, which manifests as our active resistance to talking about slavery, mentioning slavery, tracing back our patterns and habits to slavery, I see us constructing yet another collective black box and locking ourselves inside it. We, the victims of slavery, blame ourselves for racism and feel shame, anxiety and depression as a result. One major attempt to distance from the trauma of slavery

CHAPTER 8 – DISMANTLING THE COLLECTIVE BLACK BOX

and racism has been through the evolved black projection process. Self-blame and feelings of vulnerability are projected onto the "other," diverting our negative feelings (our black shadows) away from the self. These "others" who bear the weight of our rejected feelings are not just people or groups of people, but collective groupings of behaviors and/or qualities that we discredit, discount and disqualify. For example, studious behavior in young black men can be demeaned and ridiculed. Slavery taught us to appreciate black men for their "athleticism" in work and breeding. Also, slavery supported the lie that blacks were intellectually inferior to whites by prohibiting slaves from being educated. Having internalized slavery's messages, we may use intelligence or the lack of athleticism to psychologically create the us/them mentality that allows one group of blacks to ostracize and exclude another black group or individual. Our human tendency to defend against the trauma of slavery is understandable and natural. We use our collective shield to keep the trauma of slavery out of our already battered psyches. But it's not helping. It's actually detrimental to our well-being to be cut off from understanding the root source of our pain.

Racism has been one long trauma, assaulting every aspect of our humanity from our comfort in our own bodies to our sexuality and spirituality. Chronic exposure to such trauma leads to irrational and distorted beliefs that reflect victims' attempts to protect themselves and make meaning of the world. The collective black box is problematic for sure, but we can understand it as an adaptation of the group to protect itself from outside threats.

Victims of childhood abuse face this same problem: how to make sense of the harm being done to them by someone they know, love and trust. In a young mind, meaning gets twisted up so that a child ends up thinking the victimizers are right or good while he/she must therefore deserve the abuse because they are wrong or bad. Since the child is now responsible for the abuse, two irrational beliefs persist: The victimizer should be protected, and the child has power and control over the situation. These distorted beliefs then serve to protect the child from overwhelming terror, and a sense of complete despair in transforming his/her situation. Similarly, African Americans try to make sense of racism by believing that white supremacy is normal and therefore correct, and individual blacks who look, act, and/or think outside the box are the problem and threat to the group. Fearful of the painful lash of the inferiority whip, we use the black collective to try to forestall its blow. We can't control the whites, but we can assert control over other blacks.

Racism makes us call into question our own sense of value and purpose. Simply put, we African Americans no longer believe in our own effectiveness. Many African American individuals never make it out of the hood because self-hatred, low self-esteem, missing confidence and the black collective combine to create a powerful mandate: "Don't even try." Inside the collective black box, we naively imagine a fence of protection.

There is power in the group, and we feel more vulnerable as individuals, so we tend to gravitate toward the perceived sense of safety and security inside the collective black box. And there are benefits: the support, sense of belonging, feeling of being understood and watched over. But the costs are high. We have to give up our individuality to the collective black box. We have to restrict our own humanity. We have to check our dreams and secret hopes at the door if they don't conform to the collective's ideas of what blacks can and can't be.

Confronting the black shadow is the only way to do what Oprah tells us: "Live your best life." Our tendency to alleviate anxiety and protect the self through the imposed collective identity is complicated and worsened by our struggle for acceptance in the dominant white society. Our unconscious preoccupation with the black shadow makes us try to pass (be acceptable) by essentially constructing black barricades to keep everyone in place. This form of defense takes a serious toll on African Americans as individuals and as a group. Living in denial, we attempt to keep the black shadow at bay through the cultural imposition of the collective identity.

Lowering the Collective Shield

Just as white America uses the black collective (judge the whole group by the behavior of one black person) to justify the myth of white superiority, African Americans use the black collective to revile and castigate its own members because of the myth of black inferiority. We seek shelter from the black shadow by raising the collective shield. The collective shield functions in much the same way as a gang does. It assumes that everyone in the collective is the same as me, and that gives members a false sense of security. If everyone in my collective reference group (gang, church, neighborhood, social class) is the same, then I don't have to feel inferior. The collective shield therefore serves a vital role in black America, but it's not the positive spirit of group unity. It's a shame-based shelter from our black shadows and the myth of black inferiority.

Taking Shelter in Group Identity

"All black people look the same."

"Black people don't ski."

"Black people can dance."

Monolithic stereotypes about "the black" are perpetuated by both black and white America and create unrealistic and unfair expectations. The one-size-fits-all model of black development has resulted in fear and anxiety, justifying global mistreatment of us as a people and black resentment of black individuals who step out of line. The difficulty for blacks is that we feel right at home with the collective because it is familiar. Individually, we aspire to be accepted for who we are. Yet, we collectively conspire to reject any deviation from the collective. Rejection between African Americans is so familiar that we simply do it without questioning what it means to our overall well-being.

We use the collective to defend against our fear of inadequacy. The black shadow causes us to see one another as a threat. That's why the group's comfort zone is challenged by individual difference. It's why the black medical technicians were threatened by overtures of friendship by the black physician. Individual fear of the black shadow is balanced with the collective shield.

"You're not black enough," 28-year-old Robert told me. "That's what I heard from family and friends because I dated white women. I dated white women because they would approach me. They would come up to me. They would start a conversation with me. I couldn't dance, so I didn't approach black women at parties. Black women sat back, waiting for the man to make the first move. I was afraid of being laughed at because I couldn't dance. So I did nothing. Now it's me accused of rejecting black women, when it started with me being afraid of being rejected by them!"

Rejecting those individuals who don't fit the group mold is extremely hurtful to the individual and harmful to the group. When we look at black men like Robert who date white women, we can judge him negatively and see his choice as a rejection of black women (and the race) without understanding what it means to him. It is through individuality that we will honor connection and commitment to each other. The group loses energy and individuals lose passion when we demand conformity. The end result is the condemnation of individuality and loss of appreciation for our own diversity and humanity. Each collective black box carries expectations of sameness and, like the myth of black inferiority, tells you who you are instead of letting you be you.

To establish themselves, cliques reject and deny the validity of other blacks. This is how cliques work: in order to create insiders, you have to identify outsiders and make them feel ashamed of being outsiders. Because we're all in the same boat, so to speak, as blacks in a racist world, we're still expected to be loyal to the larger black collective, even while we're rejecting one another to assuage our self-hate. We end up feeling anger, depression, hostility, more self-hate, rigidity, apathy and reactivity. The potential for genuine connection is exiled to the background as we endeavor to cleanse ourselves of the black shadow.

Racism has been an occupational hazard for African Americans. Seeking respite, we created boundaries and distinctions to try to distinguish ourselves as different from "nigger" and escape our inferior blackness. Instead, we resurrected disenfranchised groups of black people, superficially joined by a particular experience or characteristic. Card-carrying members learned to behave according to group stereotypes, resulting in mass resentment between the various factions.

When I was an undergraduate at Howard University, the AKA Sorority was reserved for light-skin girls. They were expected to act "uppity" because of their middle-class backgrounds. Dark girls from lower-class backgrounds knew not to try to become an AKA. In those days, the sororities and fraternities were a lot like the ones depicted in Spike Lee's movie *School Daze*. Today, we carry class cards that come with stereotyped behavior and cause us to resent one another. For example, lower-class blacks are supposed to act "nigger-ish" and middle-class blacks are supposed to act white-ish, and we're supposed to resent each other. Within each class there may be further divisions based on skin color, neighborhood, financial status, etc.

Respecting black individuality will help each of us to acquire a greater sense of our personal worth. Then we might realize that these old adaptive responses from slavery only reinforce racism.

Good Blacks Bad Blacks

The measure of who is a good black and who is a bad black goes back to slavery, as we discussed in Chapter 1. Good blacks try not to act too black, while bad blacks act more "nigger." With each group focused negatively on the other, who is critiquing white supremacy? Addressing internalized black inferiority and healing is both an ethical imperative and a moral obligation for African Americans. We owe it to the many millions who died dreaming of freedom. We owe it to the land of our birth, where great black men and women stood proud. We owe it to the black pioneers who ran away, risking life, limbs and permanent family bonds to be free. We owe it to ourselves. And we owe it to the many millions of black children yet to be born.

Hope is essential to healing and change. Using strategies that don't work only assaults our sense of hope and leaves us frustrated. If we persist in trying to resolve the problem of white supremacy by ostracizing and excluding one another, we will not heal as a people.

Slavery disrupted our self-development and core value system. Without engaging in self-blame and group-blame, we need to understand how our lives have been disrupted and reclaim our stolen selves. All black people are made vulnerable by the "good black - bad black" split. It is self-hate that we wrestle with, struggle against, defend, hide and protect in our black collective boxes. We haven't been able to maintain a consistent sense of ourselves as deserving of life, love, prosperity and happiness. As a result, we develop destructive entitlement (you owe me) or no sense of entitlement (I don't deserve).

We want to be happy. We want to be able to love ourselves and love one another and feel welcomed and valued in the world. We want to be viewed first and foremost as unique human beings brimming with gifts to share with the rest of humanity. The white-dominated world is missing out on our brilliance and beauty, blinded by racism and the myth of black inferiority. We can't force white society to accept us, but we can develop self-acceptance. We are good enough. We don't have to dislike anyone for that to be true.

Self acceptance starts with awareness of our emotional needs so we can feel connected to ourselves and partners, family and the community. Rather than withdrawing into pain, we can reach out with compassion to African Americans and others wounded by oppression. And holding this connection, we can allow ourselves finally to feel the strong emotions that have been dangerous for us since we were taken into bondage as slaves. I believe that one reason African Americans don't want to talk about slavery is because it evokes strong emotions, and we're afraid to feel the grief. We think it is better not to think about it, but our black shadows remember, and our bodies bear the stress of what we try not to feel. It comes out in our struggles with obesity, high blood pressure, heart disease, diabetes and more.

Even the slaves couldn't talk about those feelings, and they experienced the violence of slavery first-hand. They used folk tales to try to describe their hopes, dreams, pain, suffering and never-ending wish for freedom. The magical verses about animals and supernatural wonders were ways of describing the horror and suffering of slavery, but they also revealed compassion, empathy and gratitude that they had survived. In some of the most moving folktales, slaves seemed to be forgiving themselves and their captors, which I find extraordinarily inspiring.

While more African Americans are turning to therapy for help with suffering from the indignities of racism, many still deny the pain. And as long as we hide away, as long as we choose silence, we will remain broken and fragmented. Like the slaves, we must construct our own stories of suffering so we can learn to forgive, creating more space to be at peace in our own lives. Only when the story is shared can we adequately grieve slavery and its racist aftermath. For that, we will need the courage to feel and stay with the pain, not bat it away with blame. Blame doesn't get us anywhere but stuck. When we stop blaming, there is hope for genuine relationships among all African Americans regardless of skin color, hair, and college degrees. With self-acceptance, we can relate to our brothers and sisters without fear of being judged inferior by association. By uncovering and forgiving our own sins, we can forgive our brothers and sisters for theirs against us.

We are here; we survive. As Mama said, "You may not always get what you want." But you can take back control of your mind, challenge the myth of black inferiority, and commit to living up to your potential. Facing the black shadow, you will discover freedom and hope.

Embracing Our Black Shadows

What should I do then? I will pray with the spirit, but I will pray with the mind also.

— 1 Corinthians 14:15

CHAPTER 8 – DISMANTLING THE COLLECTIVE BLACK BOX

Shadows can act on us in terrible ways when we ignore them, but if we listen to our black shadows and hear what they're whispering in our heads day and night, we can actually use that information to develop a deeper understanding of ourselves. Our black shadows hurt us when we're unconscious, but they can actually *help us* when we're conscious of what they're telling us.

What do we hear when we listen to our black shadows? We hear ourselves believing the lie of black inferiority. What do we see when we bring the black shadow into the light? We see how that lie drains us of our energy and optimism, divides us from one another, and makes it very difficult for us to muster the strength to combat racism. When we understand how we're being shadowed all the time by this racist negativity, we can choose to live our lives differently. We can stop oppressing ourselves with wrong beliefs. We can clear a new path to healing and live happy, emotionally connected, authentic lives. Once you acknowledge the black shadow in your life, you can decide whether you'll let it continue to be a negative force. You can decide to change your relationship to it and not let it influence your decisions and relationships. You can free up the energy the black shadow has been draining away and use it to deepen your consciousness, critical thinking, creativity and soul.

We don't have to be locked in constant combat with our black shadows. We can instead learn to use it as a tool for our enlightenment and understanding. Every time I hear my black shadow, I'm grateful because it reminds me not to get hooked by the lie of black inferiority in that moment. I hear my black shadow and I take a mental step back and get clarity, change my thinking. The black shadow has done you harm in the past, but now that you see it, it can't hurt you the way it once did. Instead, it can teach you to be mindful of the subtle ways we're still caught up in the emotional tangle of post-slavery trauma and still controlled by the myth of black inferiority.

The black shadow has sabotaged our aspirations and fed on our souls, leaving us poor in spirit. But now that we see it, now that we name it, it can be the catalyst for inner peace. Looking at the black shadow head-on, we can finally stop blaming ourselves and we can finally heal from the greatest betrayal of humankind: the enslavement and dehumanization of black people.

All that I wish for me, I wish for you.

Exercises for Collective Change

There are things you can do right now to take the black shadow out of the shadows and bring it into your conscious mind. You can start by talking about the residual effects of slavery in the black community. Invite someone you love and respect to have regular conversations on the following topics and explore your black shadows together.

Topic 1: *Internalized black inferiority makes us accept the idea that we're fundamentally inadequate.* Do you think this is true in your life? If so, how does it manifest? (For example, self-image, educational patterns, beliefs and attitudes about being black, family divisions, how you raise children, etc.)

Topic 2: *Black male-female relationships are still affected by slavery's images of us as unfit marriage partners.* What are some examples you can think of that support or don't support this statement? How do you think black male-female relationships could benefit from examining slavery's legacy? What can we teach our children now so they don't continue to recreate negative relationship patterns?

Topic 3: *Internalized black inferiority creates disunity in our community.* Which collective black boxes do you identify with? How have you been limited by your allegiance to a certain black group? What would it take to bring our community together? What are you willing to do to reach out, and to overcome your biases toward other blacks based on skin color, class, etc?

Topic 4: *It's time to change the focus in our community (and in the wider world) from black inferiority to white racism.* Think about the past week. What did you hear, read or say that reinforced the idea that blacks are the problem rather than white supremacy being the root cause of our problems? How did it make you feel? If you could respond to it, what would you say?

Topic 5: *My black shadow told me today____.* Now that you're hearing your own black shadow, what have you noticed it telling you? How did it change your thinking the moment you recognized it? What do you think now?

Conscious Remembrance

See them running,

no time to catch their breath.

Barking hounds turned musicians play

a loud farewell.

Witness—mind-witness dogs crazy from

the hunt, and slave catchers crazier still

from the smell of nigger.

Run slave run!

The pounding of a heartbeat silenced

by the cracking whip.

And as the ax comes closer to the

runaway foot, the ring of freedom grows

louder.

Freedom!

Run slave run!

Run, blend, bend.

Fold into the river,

all the way to freedom.

Quiet.

Hide.

Quick.

CHAPTER 1 – THE N-WORD AND THE BLACK SHADOW

In the bush.

Behind the tree.

Shhhhhh!

Fear is talking.

Fear of being a slave.

Caught – forever in the body of nigger.

Sweet, sweet darkness, cover me.

One more day.

The train's gonna come.

Underground.

No smoke, no noise.

Over the line to freedom.

Nigger magic rejected, bring back

the black man, woman, and child.

Awake!

—MFW

About the Author

Marlene F. Watson is the former Chair and Associate Professor in the Couple and Family Therapy Department at Drexel University in Philadelphia. A licensed couple and family therapist with a private practice, she was the first couple and family therapist ever to receive the prestigious Robert Wood Johnson Health Policy Fellowship. A former columnist for *Heart & Soul Magazine,* she was raised in the Philadelphia area, where she still lives. Marlene is a collector of African and African American art and she delights in mentoring African American and multi-racial young adults. She tries to live by the words of Rev. Martin Luther King, Jr: "If I can help somebody as I pass along – then my living will not be in vain."

For more information and a free Study Guide, please visit
www.drmarlenefwatson.com

Made in the USA
Middletown, DE
04 November 2014